Live each day
with inspiration!

Aileen Miga
March '06

Inspired Wealth

Financial Leadership for the 21st Century

Inspired Wealth

Financial Leadership for the 21st Century

By Aileen Miga, CFP *and Janice Hughes,* DC, LCP(hon)

INSPIRED WEALTH
Brantford, Ontario

Published by INSPIRED WEALTH.
245 King George Road, Suite 187
Brantford, ON N3R 7N7
Tel: (519) 755-9339
Email: amiga@inspiredwealth.com

Printed in the United States of America

First Edition

ISBN: 0-9734501-0-X

Designed by Graham Graphics

I dedicate this book with love and gratitude to my family: to Stan for helping me discover my path; to my parents Ursula and Henry for believing and teaching me faith; and especially to my daughters Alexandra and Katherine, who inspire me daily to keep climbing my mountain.

— Aileen

"How we live one day is how we live our lives." — *Buddha*

This simple truth allows me each day to show up and play full out. I am blessed to share these days with my husband Dave. With his patience and love we are bringing these same truths to our sons, Robert, Jackson and Kobi. My wish is to go forth and live each day fully, as if it was the last!

— Janice

Acknowledgements

They say it takes a village to raise a child; the same is true in writing a book. Without the vision and support of others this book may not have materialized. We would like to express our sincere gratitude to our editor John Stevens for seeing the potential for this work and helping us fine-tune the *12 Principles for Financial Leadership*. We would also like to thank Sarah Graham of Graham Graphics for instantly understanding the nature of this project and helping us take this book from vision to paper. Her professionalism and eye for detail in design and layout have been instrumental in creating our desired finished product.

On the idea side, we owe a debt of gratitude to many people who have helped evolve our ideas about financial leadership. We would like to acknowledge contributions both in the worlds of coaching and financial planning. Janice has been guided in her coaching career through the influence of many wonderful people involved with Coach University. She was fortunate to study under Thomas Leonard, the developer of the coaching profession, as he founded and created Coachville and many unique and wonderful programs. Aileen would like to acknowledge her friends at the Sudden Money Institute and the Nazrudin Project for providing a forum of exchange on the deeper issues about money in our lives. Aileen also extends her gratitude to her colleagues at Berkshire Investment Group, her friends and her family for their feedback and support throughout this project.

We are deeply grateful to our clients, who embraced our enthusiasm for this work and through their experiences have helped us shape *Inspired Wealth* into a workable framework and effective process. Their openness to these concepts was an essential element in the development of this book.

We acknowledge all people who are attracted and pulled to the idea of intentionally using money to achieve their highest goals. We welcome you as fellow travelers on the journey.

Table of Contents

"The only certain thing about the future is that it will surprise even those who have seen furthest into it."

— E. J. Hobsbawm

The Quest for Inspired Wealth - A Journey of Self-Discovery

We live in the most affluent society in human history, yet we lack the wisdom to use money intentionally to achieve our highest goals.

Inspired Wealth is a guide that takes individuals to a new level of interaction with money, leading to a more balanced life and the fulfillment of meaningful life goals. This is a journey through mountainous terrain; there are challenges and breathtaking vistas, unexpected opportunities and bridges to carry us across seemingly impassable chasms.

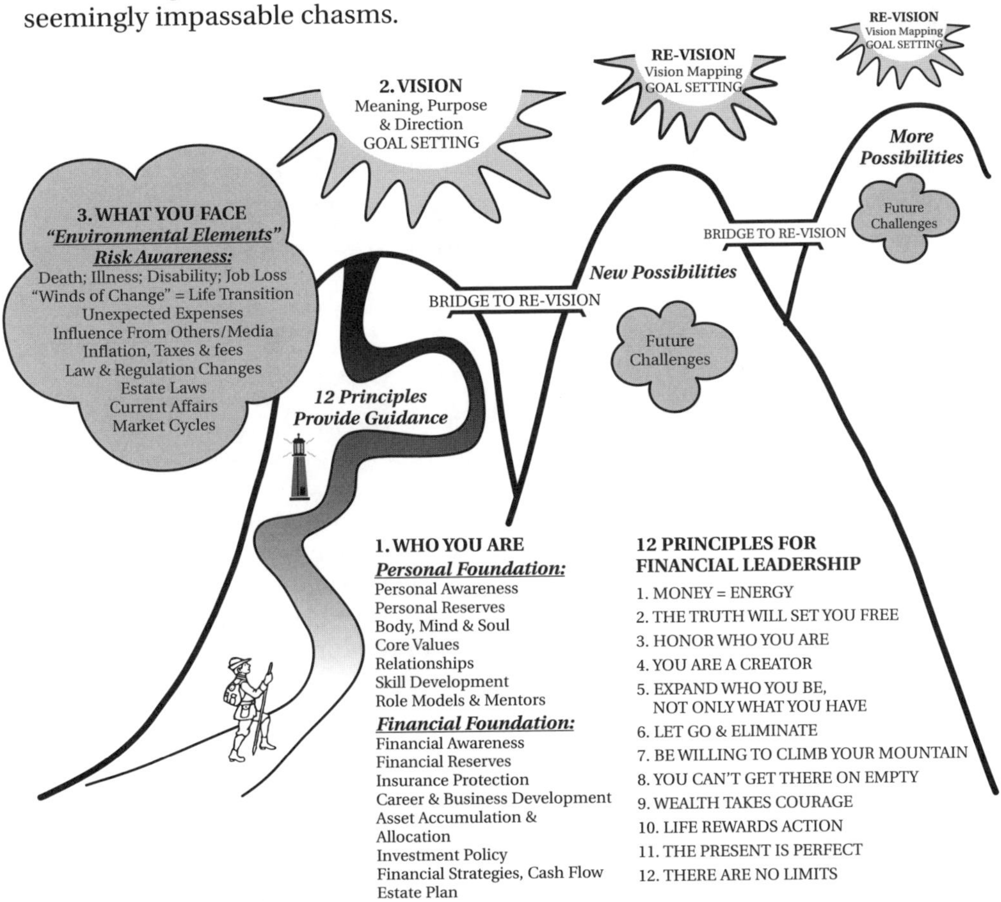

While most of us are taught to think about wealth creation as calculated, linear and primarily quantitative in approach, a closer look at how wealth is created makes one thing abundantly clear: **wealth comes from within**. Our capacity for wealth creation resides in our character, beliefs and attitudes.

We believe: You can't talk about wealth creation without talking about personal evolution. Taking your financial situation to the next level will require that you delve in and investigate who you are and how to realize your true potential. What most observers fail to see, and what we hope this book will teach you, is that the quest for wealth involves more than meets the eye. Creating wealth from the inside out is a journey of self-discovery that demands each of us become leaders - willing to explore and nurture the seeds of our own greatness.

The Quest for Inspired Wealth

Throughout the book you will find reports from those who have traveled this path before. Every individual's path is unique, but the experience of others can guide and inspire us when we are facing our own challenges.

Abraham Maslow believed that actualization was the driving force of human personality, a concept he captures in his 1954 book, *Motivation and Personality.*

"A musician must make music, an artist must paint, a poet must write, if he is to be ultimately at peace with himself. What a man can be, he must be."

More than ever, our basic needs for food and shelter are met. We have more discretionary money than ever before and we also have more choices to make than ever before. Choices about money require knowledge and the wisdom to apply this knowledge appropriately in our lives. Knowledge is easily acquired by processing information, but where do we get our wisdom about money? Will we learn it from our parents? They did not experience money in the same context we do today.

Is there a set of time-tested principles that can be applied to money? Can we live by these principles, demonstrate them for our children, teaching our children and grandchildren to make appropriate decisions about money, regardless of the way money may look tomorrow? We believe the *12 Principles for Financial Leadership* are these principles. Learning them and using them as a framework for making decisions about money, and for the purpose of communicating and teaching "inner aspects" of our money decisions, can help people attain these highest goals.

"It is not the strongest of the species that survives, nor the most intelligent, but rather the one most responsive to change."

— Charles Darwin, "The Origin of the Species," 1859

Inspired Wealth: Financial Leadership for the 21st Century is primarily a book about leading yourself, because we believe this is the first step to leading others. However, the 12 principles described here are universal and can be applied to individuals, families, corporations or even countries. Financial leadership is about becoming your own visionary and using your money intentionally with meaning, purpose and direction. The key to true vision is embracing the change we know is inevitable; aspiring to change with it; and maintaining our ability to add value regardless of the challenges: becoming "more," not "less," as a result of the change.

Who Are Aileen Miga and Janice Hughes?

We are two professionals from very different backgrounds. Yet what we have discovered is that we are two very similar people, both on a path of exploration. This path is leading us deeper into knowledge about who we are, and what we are here to do.

Dr. Janice Hughes is a Chiropractor who focuses on wellness - integrating mind, body and spirit. On her quest to find more tools and ways to help others, she discovered the profession of coaching. After hiring her own coach she began to discover who she truly is, not simply her role as a professional. She went on to train as a coach, and integrated this into her personal and professional life. By the laws of attraction she began to connect with likeminded people on their own paths of discovery. After coaching thousands of clients, Janice has grown to understand how pivotal money issues are in peoples' lives.

And then Aileen Miga entered the picture, to challenge and inspire Janice to take her coaching to the next level.

Aileen is a Certified Financial Planner™ and wealth coach. Early in her career Aileen realized that money is *never* just about money. More and more Aileen began to see that helping people achieve *sustainable* financial success demands a beyond-the-numbers approach. Through her financial planning practice, Aileen learned that leading people to understand their behavior about money is as important as showing them the numbers. She realized that effective financial planning requires integrating increased personal awareness with greater financial literacy, and this ultimately leads to greater financial resources. As a trained specialist in sudden wealth and inherited wealth issues Aileen understands the need to help people create the "legs beneath their wealth." She believes the key to sustainable wealth creation involves moving the whole person forward, not just their finances. Focusing on the technical side of money is not enough: the greater challenge is to know our "self" well enough to make optimal choices about money, which work to support, not sabotage, our efforts.

Her search for effective ways to help people make better choices with money led her to explore a holistic approach to financial planning. For Aileen, this meant finding a way to help people understand where they are, where they would like to be, and how to map out their individual paths to support them in getting there. Helping people learn to use money intentionally became her calling.

She began to change her financial-planning practice to implement this holistic approach and immediately discovered that there were very few tools available within the financial planning profession to help her teach clients to use money more intentionally. Aileen began to search out like-minded individuals with whom she could share her vision.

After meeting Dr. Hughes Aileen knew immediately she had found someone who could help her create the tools she needed to build the holistic financial planning practice she envisioned.

One of the first things Dr. Hughes taught Aileen was the principle of attraction. It became clear to both that they were drawn to one another for a reason. As Aileen began to share her vision with Janice it became obvious that their work covered a lot of common ground. Both were trying to help clients achieve their greatest potential. As a coach, Janice would regularly help clients explore their attitudes and habits around money issues. As a financial planner Aileen found herself coaching clients to examine their beliefs and change their behaviors around money. Together they envisioned creating a framework, which would lead people to a new level of connection with their money: to help people achieve true wealth and attain their highest goals.

And so was born the quest for inspired wealth. To answer the questions:

- How to make sense of all the information about money
- How to reduce its complexity and create real value with knowledge in the context of our individual lives - in a way that expands us and fulfills our desire to live richer, more intentional lives
- How to use money intentionally - with meaning, purpose and direction

This is the mission of ***Inspired Wealth: Financial Leadership for the 21st century.***

The Call to Adventure

You are holding this book in your hands because you know there is more to life, and to handling money, than the old well-traveled road of getting and spending. This book will take you on a journey through an adventurous landscape of self awareness. Everything is new and fresh - and much is unexpected. Old enemies turn out to be allies, insurmountable obstacles become bridges to a fuller life. This is the world of inspired wealth and your path takes you through the very heart of a vast, richly varied landscape. You are going to need courage on this journey; the courage to let go of old ways of looking at life and money, and the courage to venture into unknown territory. Fear Not! You have on your side two experienced guides who have themselves taken the journey and have proven they know the way.

Aileen and Janice will be at your side on your first exploration of this new world, and they will leave in your hands the tools and knowledge that will enable you to negotiate whatever challenges you meet. Their fundamental toolkit consists of the *12 Principles for Financial Leadership*, which will be a powerful source of inspiration and guidance on your journey.

This is a great opportunity to discover and get to know yourself in a new way - as an adventurer, the hero of your own success story.

Your Inspired Wealth Journal

When people embark on a journey, they often find it valuable to keep a journal. We encourage you to use a notebook to do the exercises in this book. As we take you through the 12 principles consider how applying them in your life can improve your finances and well-being.

We promise not to ask you to write down everything you spend. However, it is often helpful to reflect and write about how money impacts your life day to day. Your Inspired Wealth Journal can help you increase your awareness and clarity about the money issues in your life and can be a valuable tool in helping you make lasting change.

Principle #1
Money = Energy

- ✓ **Energy: The ability to get work done**
- ✓ **A symbol of appreciation**
- ✓ **Flows to those who add value**
- ✓ **You can raise your energy to attract more**

When was the last time you thought about money?

Was it an hour ago? 20 minutes ago? 2 minutes ago?

If we are honest with ourselves, we will admit we spend an inordinate amount of time thinking about money: how much we have or don't have, how to repay what we owe or invest what we've accumulated, or simply how to get some more!

In today's society more than ever before, money touches every aspect of our lives.

Never before has money been so pervasive in our lives and so complicated. Today we have more options about how to spend, save and invest our money than ever before:

more options, **more demands**, **more messages** and **more confusion.**

As a result of the challenges money presents, one of the greatest financial aspirations of many has become simply "not to have to think about money." You've probably said it yourself on occasion: " I wish I didn't have to think about money." It's a common fantasy.

Not thinking about money would suit us just fine. Yes... then we would be able to escape the many contradictions and paradoxes that money presents. But have you tried it lately? Have you really tried not thinking about money? How long did you last?

For most of us, it's impossible to escape thinking about money for any extended period of time. So how about letting go of the notion that we shouldn't think too much about money, that it's not polite or politically correct. Instead, we suggest you acknowledge that money is an extremely powerful force in your life and trust that if it is so inherently powerful, it's futile to wish you didn't have to think about it. What if you replaced this escapism with awareness and began to deepen your understanding about what money is and what it can really do for you.

What comes to mind when you think about money?

The two most common ways we comprehend money are through numbers and feelings:

Through numbers, amounts:

- Account balances
- Mortgages
- Income
- Net worth
- Bills, prices

Through feelings:

- Inadequacy, fear, sorrow, anger, resentment, guilt, become overwhelm
- Excitement, gratitude, pride, accomplishment, generosity, joy, security

Thinking about money solely in terms of numbers keeps it separate from our self-worth, and keeps us from internalizing its essence. We know that money is about more than numbers.

Thinking about money mainly in terms of how we feel about it is also limiting. How we feel about money certainly has an impact on how we experience it in our lives. Exploring our feelings around money can be enlightening; it can help us make appropriate spending and investment decisions. However, our feelings sometimes get in the way of making sound financial decisions. If feelings are our primary way of relating to money, it can be difficult to deal with it intentionally and objectively.

We propose a third, much more powerful and effective way of understanding money:

Money = Energy

Money is a natural resource. This is a new idea that is also very old, probably one of the oldest ways of understanding money. Money is currency. The root word of currency is current, meaning movement or flow, as of a river or an electrical charge. This offers us a more dynamic understanding of money; it circulates, it can be converted from one form to another, as the current in a river can be converted to electrical current in a power-generating station. If money is the current, we are the conduit: it flows through us and we direct its use.

Money is the fuel
You are the vehicle
Your goals are the road
Your life is the terrain
Your vision is the destination

There is great power in understanding that money is currency. We can deal in dollars, pebbles or barter; all are ways of exchanging energy. To attract more, we can change the focus and intensity of what we do to earn this currency.

We can create more value to attract more money. Although we may know this intellectually, it seems that most people have not been able to master the money forces in their lives. The reason is the constellation of conflicting thoughts and emotions we carry around money. In order to broaden and deepen our relationship with money, each of us must investigate money and its meaning in our own lives. Because we are all individuals, your particular combination of money experiences, beliefs and values is unique to you.

Congealed Energy

We like to say money is congealed energy; it is one of the primary means of supplying the energy needed to transform and solidify ideas and intentions into reality. Money of course is not the only energy required for successful transformations of ideas and intentions. Others include: vitality (health), love (support and inspiration), determination and imagination (creativity).

Our Multi-dimensional Connection With Money

Finding truly effective solutions to the challenges of money in our lives requires that we become aware of our multi-dimensional connection with money. Each of our dimensions is affected by our choices. Coming to understand how to choose with money in ways that support your whole being is a breakthrough that will help you sustain wealth and improve well-being. Money is energy we use to express what we think, what we can shoulder, what we feel/love. It flows through us, through mind, body and spirit and its end use is shaped by our inner dynamics.

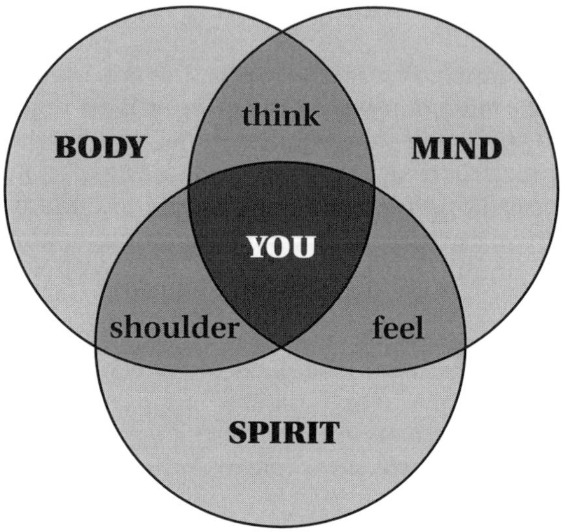

How often do we make choices about money that disregard our physical, mental and spiritual needs? How effective are our choices if a solution in one area creates a problem in another?

The Great Energy Swap

All of our financial transactions can be reduced to an exchange of energy. We freely exchange our money for the energy of others when we feel they have something of value to offer us. When we use someone else's energy to get work done, we pay them money. Consider the simple example of getting the lawn mowed. We can reduce our own physical efforts by changing the way we do the work - say using a gas or electric lawnmower to lighten the workload of cutting the lawn. We can also exchange the workload for money with the kid down the street, who will be delighted to trade his physical energy (which he likely has plenty of) for the potential energy of cash to spend (which he likely wants more of). This results in a trade of energy: each person trades what they have (the kid has physical energy and time, the adult has money) for what they need (the kid needs money, the adult needs physical energy and time). This is a simple example. However, all money transactions follow the same logic: all are an exchange of one form of energy for another. Thus we believe the very best definition of money, the one with the most meaning and possibility, is that money is a form of energy: the ability to get work done.

Money Connects Us

We are taught to compete for money. Yet it is clearly more effective to see money as something that connects us, rather than something that separates us. It is a symbol of appreciation for the value we add. This can be a powerful paradigm shift that can help you clarify how to create more wealth in your life. Seeing money as something that connects us with one another has significant implications personally, in business, socially and even geopolitically. Applying this principle to your life can help you improve the way you understand and use money. It can open you up to new possibilities by helping you see opportunities to add value in every area of your life.

Take a look at your own example. How does the money you receive from the value you add connect you to others? If you've started your own business, how does your new enterprise and your profits impact your community? If you work for a large corporation, how does the value you add impact the corporation's bottom-line, and what impact does this have on the economy and eventually your salary? If you're working in the home, how does your work support others who are then able to attract money? In raising children, how does your parenting shape your children, and how does this add value to society? How does what we teach children today increase their capacity to add value to others in exchange for money tomorrow? How does the money you spend shopping connect you to others? Why do you choose to reward one brand or product over another? What added value are you willing to exchange more of your money for? How could improving your financial situation impact others? How could your having financial problems impact others?

Do you see how money connects us all? We are all connected through the value we add to one another. **If you wish to attract more money you will need to figure out how to increase or improve the focus of your own energy (physical, mental, creative, etc.) and create more value to add to others.** This is a core dynamic in the spirit of innovation; it's how we attract money. Your ability to use this concept can lead you to see and honor the true value, or the potential value, of your unique abilities. Unique abilities are simply the things you do best that provide the most value to others. Knowing what they are can help you stay focused on the best way to add value to others, and consequently attract more money with greater ease.

"It is one of the most beautiful compensations of this life that no man can sincerely try to help another without helping himself."

— Ralph Waldo Emerson

An Inspiring View of Money:

- **Money is symbol of appreciation, a gesture of goodwill**
- **Taking care of your prosperity is paying attention to the energy reserves that you need to get work done, to fulfill your life purpose or calling**
- **Money flows to those who give more in use value than they give in cash value. Money flows based on the exchange of energy. If we give more value to others the natural flow is to attract more energy to us, in the form of money, vitality or some other form of energy.**

Exercise - ***Money is Energy***

Before you set out on your journey, it will be important that you clearly grasp what has drawn you to the adventure. What do you want your money to do for you? To bring this into focus we invite you to copy the sentence below into your Inspired Wealth Journal and fill in the blank as fully and specifically as you can. This will help you put aside your old ways for the new and exciting pathways of the Inspired Wealth Quest.

Since I see money as a form of energy (the ability to get work done), I want

my money to____ for me."

Some of our clients' responses:

- I want my money to make my life easier - less work and stress for me.
- I want my money to protect those I love from the pain of financial hardship.
- I want my money to allow me to experience travel with the confidence that I can afford it.
- I want my money to enable me to say yes freely to projects that excite me.
- I want my money to facilitate a richer experience of life.
- I want my money to allow me to take more risks with greater safety in the direction of my dreams.
- I want my money to expand the human capital of each member of my family so we can all discover our potential.

Reflect on your own answer: do you want your money to help you move toward something or away from something? Are you creating or escaping? Is what you want your money to do for you sustainable, does it honor your whole being: body, mind and soul? Does it increase your capacity to add value to others?

Aileen:

When I work with clients on a financial plan, I help them create a "Money Filter." This is a sentence, which clarifies what they want their money to do for them. For example, Samantha and Rick's money filter was: "We want our money to enable us to have meaningful life experiences with confidence." This statement became the filter through which their decisions about money passed. It was particularly eye opening for them to measure their spending in this way. Was what they were spending their family's resources on bringing them more meaningful experiences and greater confidence? In many cases it was not. The money filter helped them focus on their intentions for money and was simple enough for them to do without much effort. They began testing all of their energy output through this filter and recognized that many of their activities were robbing them of the time and resources to pursue more meaningful experiences in life. More than that, the experiences that they were having were often undermined by the insecurity they felt by their weakening financial situation. This new awareness lead the couple to understand how important a strong financial foundation was to their ability to "have meaningful life experiences with confidence." The result was that saving money became easier for Samantha and Rick, because they realized that feeling confident was more important to them than having "more."

Think of all the ways you spend money: which items enable you to do things that are meaningful for you (and have a high return of energy); that compound your ability to get meaningful work done? Conversely, which items hold little meaning for you and lead to an energy drain?

The Climber's Voice:

"One day I realized I wanted to climb a mountain. This desire grew quietly, initially in the form of a faint whisper from a deep place within my soul. It sort of came out of the blue, but once I heard it, I knew it was a need to learn more about who I was and what I was made of: my heart, my character, my commitment. The decision to climb was pivotal in my life. I can only explain the feeling as a deep desire to feel fully alive. Intuitively, I knew that whatever it cost me in time, energy and money to listen to this voice, it was going to be far less than what I stood to gain. I knew that if I could do this one thing - I could do anything, and that this experience would increase my capacity to add value to everything I did after that."

Now that you understand that money is energy, the remaining principles will teach you financial leadership *from within:* they will guide you in using money intentionally to create the life you desire.

Principle #2
The Truth Will Set You Free

- ✓ **In All Learning Knowing Where to Begin is Essential**
- ✓ **Internal Integrity is an Opportunity**
- ✓ **Learn the Truth About Your Money**

To achieve your goals and dreams you will need to take a close look at your starting place. Without a truthful understanding of your financial foundation, you could set out with vital pieces missing and undermine the success of the entire journey. This is an opportunity to find truth and authenticity with respect to your money and your being, and it's an essential part of equipping yourself appropriately for the road ahead.

The Truth Will Set You Free

While it sounds like an old cliché, this well-known principle is rich with wisdom. Embracing truth is an opportunity to explore all areas of your life. Taking an in-depth look at your present existing financial circumstances helps you identify potential roadblocks and reduce the risks that are predicable and avoidable. You will benefit by clarifying where your personal and financial foundation can be strengthened to increase the likelihood of achieving your goals. Once you gather the data and clarify the truth about your circumstances you will be free to act with greater confidence.

When we ignore what we know is true, the cost is often more than we can afford.

Remember Enron?

Here is a famous example of what not facing the truth about money can lead to. At Enron it became obvious that their business model did not produce the earnings results that were expected. But because top executives didn't want to face the truth about their company's earnings they continued working with a broken model. They hid the truth and the deception compounded. Had the leaders recognized the truth early enough and understood how disaster multiplies from not telling the truth, they could have made the changes and the shifts required. This is where leadership was needed, and was sorely lacking. What did hiding the truth **cost** the executives at Enron?

The Truth about Your Assets and Liabilities

Let's begin by taking a closer look at your current situation. Below is an exercise that will help you shed some light on the state of your financial foundation and on your *whole being*. We call this the **Inspired Balance Sheet**. It's a tool that expands on an integral part of financial planning: the balance sheet, also known as the net worth statement. In helping you create sustainable wealth, our approach is to include your whole life because we want you to succeed in all aspects of your life, so there are categories here you won't find anywhere else. The nonfinancial assets and liabilities are the other energies in your life and the values that give your life meaning.

The following is an example with sample nonfinancial assets and liabilities filled in - yours may be different. Please list your own nonfinancial assets and liabilities in your journal using this format. Then begin monitoring your *whole* Inspired Balance Sheet.

Inspired Balance Sheet

Assets		**Liabilities**	
Cash	$ __________	CreditCard Debt	$ __________
Investments	$ __________	Investment Loans	$ __________
Real Estate	$ __________	Mortgages	$ __________
Vehicles	$ __________	Car Loans	$ __________
Personal	$ __________	Consumer Loans	$ __________
Toys	$ __________		
Total	**$ __________**	**Total**	**$ __________**

Assets	Liabilities
Time	No Time
Health	Unhealthy Patterns
Relationships	Rackets
Skills	Dependencies and Addictions
Creativity	Bad Stress
Knowledge	Helplessness
Wisdom	Ignorance
Passion	Apathy
Values	Hopelessness
Simplicity	Complexity
Confidence	Self-doubt
Personal Integrity	Incongruencies
Clarity	Confusion
etc.	etc.

Quantitative vs. Non-Quantitative Assets and Liabilities

In the financial context **assets** refer to all of your property, financial investments, and other financial resources. These are generally things that are easily measured (quantitative). We look at an investment statement and we instantly know the value of our holdings. However, in addition to our quantitative assets we also have many **non-quantitative assets**. These assets cannot be measured in a traditional way, but they can be extremely valuable. In the course of your lifetime, your non-quantitative assets are essential elements that determine your ability to create and maintain real wealth.

Liabilities, on the other hand, are your financial obligations or debts: they include mortgages, car loans, personal loans, credit card balances, and deferred income taxes. Our concept of liabilities should be expanded to also include: our fears, our limiting beliefs, behaviors which are inconsistent with our goals, etc. These are all liabilities, which tend to limit our ability to create and maintain lasting wealth.

The Inspired Balance Sheet is a Tool to Help You Live a Balanced Life

> **"For everything you have missed, you have gained something else."**
>
> — *Ralph Waldo Emerson*

Often we tend to focus so hard on what we don't have that we miss out on what we do have. You can choose to stop doing this to yourself. You can live your life more fully and more honestly by taking a look at all that you DO have in your life. There is no sense in lamenting over the road not taken. Where you have been was essential to get you to where you are today. And where you are today is the platform from which you will launch tomorrow. Be grateful for all that you have and all that you are NOW and choose to use your gifts in a meaningful way to create the life you want.

If you look beneath the surface of the negative events that have occurred in your life, you will often find that there were benefits to your having been through them. What have you learned from your struggles? How have they made you stronger? You can turn negative experiences into assets by embracing the lessons they teach you.

> **"When one door closes, another opens; but we often look so long and so regretfully upon the closed door that we do not see the one which has opened for us."**
>
> ***— Alexander Graham Bell***

In assessing how you are using your money, what matters most is that you are using your resources to continually increase your financial and nonfinancial assets and decrease your liabilities. What we'd like you to see clearly is that there is more to wealth than just the financial dimension. One of the most interesting lessons about money is that people often sacrifice so much in acquiring it, that once they have the money they feel a sense of emptiness. Only then do they realize the value of what they had given up for money. One of the greatest challenges that many financially successful people face today is to find meaning in their lives. They feel fortunate but not fulfilled.

In This Way Sometimes More is Less, and Sometimes Winning is Losing

Janice:
I can attest to this one! I had a full life, a busy and fulfilling practice, a great relationship with my husband, a growing and inquisitive son, professional recognition sitting on several boards and involved with decision makers in my profession. I had the great building blocks in place. Financially, we had covered all our bases, and were beginning to create a wealth plan. Yet I kept waking up asking if this was all there was. Was the making of money and accumulating "stuff" all there was to life? It was at this point that I began to ask the questions about what brought me value.

Through asking myself stronger questions, I began to change the "successful practice." We decided to have more children, to change my hours so that I had more time with the family. I brought in a wonderful associate to mentor, who would eventually purchase my practice. I had more creativity in my life, more fulfillment and satisfaction, and I also began to open up to new projects and ideas. These opportunities in turn have developed into new sources of energy, money and fulfillment.

Take a look at the list of nonfinancial assets on your Inspired Balance Sheet and reflect on how precious all of these things are. You can expand how you think about wealth by simply including these in your definition of assets. Not only does this make you feel *rich*, it also is a better indicator of your personal potential.

When you look at your nonfinancial liabilities, understand that energy drains take away from your wealth. Just as the nonfinancial assets are more precious than money, the nonfinancial liabilities can be more problematic than your financial liabilities.

The Family Balance Sheet:

Most of us live in the context of our family, so we also need to make sure this snapshot includes the Family Balance Sheet. There are four types of capital in families:

1) Human Capital - the individual family members are and what they are called to do;
2) Intellectual Capital - how family members learn, communicate, and make joint decisions;
3) Social Capital - how family members engage society at large;
4) Financial Capital - the property of the family.

Families that enhance human, intellectual, and social capital have a better chance of growing great human beings.

"Your family's greatest assets are the human potential of each of its members."

— Charles W. Collier; Wealth in Families

To get a better understanding of your family's wealth you must consider the future (potential) value of your family's human, intellectual and social capital. For example, a university graduate might have a negative financial net worth, but the present value of his or her human capital might be $3 million in terms of earnings. Some forms of human, intellectual and social capital are difficult to measure. Parents who, through their own process of self discovery, encourage their children to seek out what makes them passionate versus what will make them money are contributing enormously to their family's and their community's human capital. It would be very difficult to put a dollar value on what they have contributed, but we know that most of the greatest contributions to society are made by people who are passionate about what they do.

Janice:
My oldest son's kindergarten class did a unit on community; the teacher had many parents from different careers and professions come in to talk to the class. I went in to talk about chiropractic and health, one dad was an engineer who worked on the railway, one mom was a nurse, another stayed at home to raise her wonderful family, etc. At the end of the unit the teacher had the children stand up and describe what they would love to be when they grow. The boy whose dad was an engineer said he would like to be a train engineer; the girl whose mother was a nurse wanted to be a nurse. All around the circle 95 percent of kids said they wanted to be what their parents were, and the others said they wanted to be what one of the other kid's parents were. She came to my son last, and he looked slowly around the circle, and then stood up. He said "I would like to be a chiropractor when I grow up... until my parents die, then I would love to be an explorer!"

As a parent, can I nurture and grow this child to explore what he would love to be, versus what I am, or what is acceptable as a career for the future? I certainly intend to!

How about considering your human capital when making decisions about work and retirement? Should you deplete your energy and vitality overworking to retire at 55, all the while not enjoying life fully. Or is it wise to take work you love, that supports your whole being and makes you well, and continue to work at what you love until 68, 70 and beyond? Could this possibly transcend the need for retirement? We are living longer, healthier lives. Anti-aging research will no doubt continue to add to this trend. What implications will this have on the decisions we make about money in our lives?

Consider Your Balance Sheet

Is your way of life sustainable?

Creating wealth while depleting our source (who we are) leads to less, not more. Our goal is to create the wealth and replenish the source. This applies to doing work you love, to socially responsible investing, to keeping balance in life and building great companies, communities and families.
Unsustainable = Expensive

Kelly knew her job was killing her spirit!
She had climbed the corporate ladder quickly in her insurance company. She was organized, energetic, and a great saleswoman. Her income soared as she accomplished more and more. Yet she was tired of working harder every step of the way. She worked 14-16 hour days, ate out late at night, and went home to regroup and come back at it again the next day. What good would her money be when she had no time to enjoy it? As it was, she never spent much time at her gorgeous home - she might as well still be living in a one bedroom apartment. Her investment portfolio was growing rapidly, even in challenging markets. Yet would she ever be able to survive at this pace to enjoy the long-term benefits of her wealth?

Kelly hired a coach. She had heard so much about life coaching through a friend that she decided working with a coach might help her get a life! The first thing her coach helped her to see was that this would be the most difficult task she had undertaken yet. She had set her goals and aspirations for her career and her life based on input from everyone around her. Because she was good at her job, she had poured all her energy into this area of her life. Now the coach was asking her to set goals and make plans for other areas of her life. This felt like work, yet without some kind of balance, how sustainable would her success be? How successful would she be?

Often what we consider truth is simply our current point of reference. How is your current reference point coloring your judgment or interpretation of events, of others, or of your investments? Ask yourself: is this The Truth or is it My Truth. Becoming aware of your point of reference and questioning its relevance to the situation is an important skill that can increase awareness and lead to wiser decisions. It enables us to recognize the opportunity to shift and look at things from a different angle, thus adding a new dimension to our ability to identify truth.

"The more you know the more you know you don't know anything."

—Albert Einstein

Some questions to ask yourself that can help clarify your point of reference in any situation that brings up emotion (positive and/or negative):

- Why do I feel this way?
- How did I come to that conclusion?
- What did I expect?
- Why did I have those expectations?
- What outcome could make me feel differently about this situation/ investment/relationship?

Since much of our point of reference is made up of our own experience, it is helpful to understand this and observe it, so that you can step over your personal history and see what can be true. What is the POTENTIAL beyond your current experience?

What You Believe About Money

Learning the truth about your relationship with money is a process of collecting data and taking stock. It requires excavating beneath the surface, a kind of personal archeological dig. We need to excavate the beliefs that influence your behavior with money. Think about your beliefs about money:

Who taught you that? Who told you that?

There is a difference between a belief and a knowing. You actually learn a belief from someone else in your life at an early age. In most cases we have never asked if this belief serves us at this point in our life. A knowing comes from you.

We'd like you to understand the source of your beliefs and attitudes about money. One of the most revealing exercises about your relationship with money is The Money Autobiography. In this exercise you recall your earliest memories of money. You revisit your personal history to better understand the money dynamics presenting themselves in your life today. Take out your journal and reflect on the questions in this exercise. This exercise is also valuable in helping you understand how the way you are with money may impact the way your children experience money in their lives....as they say, "An ounce of prevention is worth a pound of cure."

Money Autobiography:

Your past holds the key to your financial future. As a child you began to form your first impressions of what money is all about:

What did your mother say about money?

How did your mother spend money, what did she spend it on?

What did your father do and say about money?

Were there arguments in your home around the topic of money and finances?

What sayings pop into your mind when we ask you about money?

What is your happiest moment with money? Your unhappiest?

What happened to family members during the depression and recessions?

How is /was the subject of money addressed by your church or the religious traditions of your relatives?

How did your family communicate about money? How does your family now communicate about money?

As a child did you feel poor or rich?

Did you long for what other children had?

Will you inherit money? How does that make you feel?

How do you feel about taxes, welfare, people living off the system?

Are you generous, overgenerous, stingy, frugal?

Do you tip, and how much?

Do you judge others by how you perceive they deal with their money?

Do you tithe, give money away?

Do you spend some, save some, and give some away? In what proportions?

Internal Integrity is an Opportunity

Internal integrity is about learning what is true and authentic for you and letting go of the beliefs about yourself that you may have *borrowed* from others, and, which may no longer serve you. You need to act on the truth that comes from you. Staying *integrated* requires that you continuously focus on the truth as it emerges and welcome it as a catalyst for further personal growth. In this way, knowing the truth about who you are presents itself as an opportunity to make the choices that are right for you. This is part of your journey toward self-discovery and an essential part of financial leadership.

Have you ever been afraid of learning the truth about something? Have you had the experience of avoiding seeking the truth only to have your fear grow? It's likely that once you chose to see the truth your fear began to dissipate.

Aileen:
As a financial advisor, I have repeatedly seen that most of the fear people feel about money stems from their simply not knowing the truth about their financial situation and not knowing themselves well enough. Learning more about what is true for you is key in freeing you from fear and helping you make better choices with money. We will address fear in great detail in another chapter; however, it is important here for you to see how it connects to truth. In our noisy world many have lost the sense of their truth, their intuitive inner being. Consequently they find it difficult to make choices that will serve them well. We want you to know your truth deeply, so that you can act with internal integrity and authenticity to make intentional use of your money with confidence and peace, instead of reacting with anxiety and fear. This is what financial planning is all about.

Here are a few points to reflect on to help you challenge what you believe about yourself, so you can begin revealing what is true for you. In asking yourself these questions, listen to your inner voice and pay attention to the images that pop up spontaneously in your mind. Allow these images to guide you toward your authentic truth.

- Challenge your false beliefs - What exactly are you so afraid of? What is keeping you from doing everything that you know you should be doing in order to reach your goal?

- Challenge the way you see yourself - we all get used to thinking and seeing ourselves in a certain way. This can limit our ability to grow because we tend to live up to our expectations of ourselves, which become self-fulfilling: If you tend to picture yourself as not creative, you will avoid opportunities where you are required to be creative. This will in turn keep your creativity dormant, and you will continue to believe that you are not creative. How can you expand your view and vision of yourself?

- Picture yourself the way you want to be. If you want to be creative, see yourself embracing the opportunity to express your creativity. Ask yourself, how do people who embrace creativity live? How do they prepare a meal, write a note, or choose a gift? Know that what you focus on expands - begin to focus on the way you want to be.

- What have you avoided doing because you have told yourself that you cannot possibly do it? Why not? Is this an excuse or is it a lack of skill or knowledge, or a fear that you feel you cannot realistically overcome?

- Assessing the data means that you realize there are no coincidences in life, we attract all that comes into our lives. Taking responsibility can be difficult but very liberating, because it means that we also have the power to manifest what we desire. Look around. Do you have the life you desire? If not, what is holding you back?

Exercise - ***Write your own eulogy. What would others say about you? What would you* like *others to say about you?***

"We are here today to celebrate the life of John. He has touched us all in many ways. As I look around I see his loving family, his children who are a reflection of his love and spirit. His children are involved in different things in life, yet all do them fully. They support and love their spouses and children, and are more focused on their development as a family versus working to accomplish more in the outside world. His wife, with whom he has lived passionately and explored greatly, is here. John's business associates are here because of the strong relationship they developed through their work connections. Many of his competitors from the business world are here, because they knew John to be a man of integrity and spirit. He was someone who called them all, and their businesses, to be excellent. Let us celebrate John's life, and the principles that he stood for. Each of us is stronger and more loving for having known John."

This was written by John in a workshop at a time of his life when his main focus and drive came from his professional life. People in the workshop described him as driven, focused, intense, business-like, cold, more focused on success than relationships. John's insights and breakthrough came when he acknowledged that he wanted to be a family man, not simply providing for his family, but actually having relationships with all members. In writing his eulogy he realized this would require change. The great thing was that his family was still young, his life still before him. He quickly acted to make changes so that even if circumstances cut short his days on earth, he could create the life that he described above!

Learn the Truth About Risk

Money, risk and reward are intimately bound together. The universe always asks what you are willing to give before it will reward you.

For instance, there are risks in living from paycheck to paycheck without any reserves. There is nothing to fall back on if the income stream is interrupted by illness, disability or any of the other accidents of life. Another risk could be not having the financial resources to pursue your dream. Your dream of starting your own business may be at risk if you never save enough money to create the reserves to allow you to quit your job with some start-up capital. These are financial risks.

There are all sorts of nonfinancial risks that threaten our sense of balance and our ability to live the life that we desire:

- Health Risks - The greatest asset you have is your health. If you are not convinced of this yet, ask someone who has lost their good health and has many unfulfilled dreams.
- The risk that your skills will become outdated if you don't keep up with change.
- The greatest risk may be coming to the end of your life and realizing that you didn't live the way you wanted, that you didn't let the world hear your music. Knowing that your music will die with you is the greatest sadness.

The Climber's Voice:

"Yes... I know how risky mountain climbing is. There was a time when I thought mountain climbers were crazy! I wondered why anyone would leave the comfort and security of flat ground to scale a mountain. Now I see that for some not climbing the mountain is a more certain risk. I am not prepared to live the rest of my life wishing I had fulfilled this dream. Instead, I'll learn what I need to so that I am well prepared for this challenge."

People over 65 were asked, "If you could live your life over, what would you do differently?" They said three things: "I'd take time to stop and ask the big questions. I'd be more courageous and take more risks in work and love. I'd try to live with purpose—to make a difference."

— Richard Leider, founding partner of the Inventure Group

The Truth About Change

The truth is that rapid change will continue to be a constant in our lives. Accepting this truth and discovering how to evolve through the changes and thereby enrich our lives is a much more effective way of living than resisting and fearing change.

This is why it's so important to know where you are at this point. Be aware of who you are, so that when you identify where you want to go you'll know what you need to do to get there. In the new economy, knowing who you are and what is constant in your life will be as important as knowing what is flexible and how to make adjustments. If you go through enough change and transition in your life, you will see that, "the more things change the more they stay the same." Perhaps because the by-product of constant change is a stronger core, an axle, upon which the variables spin. Change can make us stronger if we let go of our fear and choose to see it that way. Our ability to change gracefully and fully adapt to new environments will depend on our ability to be grounded by strong core values that permeate all that we do. The combination of our own unique blend of core values combined with our "way" is what adds value to all our endeavors.

Are You Prepared for the Inevitable Change?

Assess the risks inherent in maintaining the status quo. Perhaps the risk of not using your resources to manifest the life that you desire is a risk you are not willing to take.

> **"Not in his goals but in his transitions is man great."**
>
> — *Ralph Waldo Emerson*

It is not the attaining of a goal that makes you a success. Rather, it is what you have learned and who you have become in the process of achieving your goal. What doubts and fears have you had to face? What obstacles made you rethink your goal and redouble your efforts? What mountains have you already climbed?

As you accept and overcome your challenges, you change, you evolve. You become stronger, wiser, and more self-confident. You are able to lead yourself and others with greater clarity. You transform beliefs into knowings. You become very aware of your personal power. You know that you are responsible for making things happen in your life. You have control of more than you once thought. This is truth. This is leadership.

We believe that the object of life is not happiness and security: it is growth. The by-product is joy.

As a final check before you pack your bags for the journey, fill in the blank in the following sentence:

The truth about money that I know I must now face is

____

____.

Principle #3
Honor Who You Are

- ✓ **Embrace your values and desires: they are part of your unique job description**
- ✓ **Use money in ways that are congruent with your values to increase fulfillment**

The resources the adventurer needs are not just material goods - on your journey you will need to know as much as possible about the resources within you - the solid foundation stones of your own unique way of being in the world.

Financial leadership begins when you awaken to the wealth and happiness that is already there. This is a choice. You can decide to be mindful and deliberate, to be conscious, be aware of your thoughts and actions and dreams instead of doing things on automatic pilot. In this chapter we will explore three vital inner resources that will make your journey meaningful and rewarding - Authentic Goals, Inner Values and Personal Vision.

"You are a very special person–become what you are."

— Archbishop Desmond M. Tutu, Nobel Peace Prize Winner

Authentic Goals

Webster's dictionary describes an objective as "pertaining to an external object or event quite independent of the observer's emotions or imagination." What we are proposing you look for is quite different. We do not want you to focus on things that are only external to you. Setting your goals from your internal imagination, from who you be on the inside, can help ensure that you are not simply trying to create a lifestyle that matches other people's lifestyle expectations. We want to enable you to set your goals according to your own inner desires, so that you are naturally pulled to achieving them. Upon accomplishing your goals you find fulfillment at a deep and core level, not simply a false and fleeting happiness. Goals defined by your culture, your friends or the wishes of others will ultimately leave you feeling very empty.

An Inspiring View of Money:

- **Remember what it was like when you thought you could do anything?**
- **Embrace your desires and "inklings."**
- **Don't let others tell you what you need to make you happy.**

Authentic goals **charge** your life plan with a compelling sense of purpose. They provide you with a higher form of energy (like high octane fuel: it's cleaner and more valuable), and they provide a sound basis for making future decisions, financial or otherwise. People who have authentic goals are positive and brimming with enthusiasm. They are passionate and fulfilled and confidently know how to choose what's right for them. This makes them naturally strong leaders.

Inner Values

To begin, let's take a look at the difference between happiness, satisfaction and fulfillment.

Have you ever tried to define happiness? Happiness can be short-lived and a fleeting state. We are happy when we get what we want, but this is a constantly moving target.

Happiness - Satisfaction - Fulfillment

Happiness - Wants

- **We are happy when we get what we want**
  - **Short-lived and fleeting**

Satisfaction - Needs

- **We are satisfied when we recognize what we need, and get our needs met**
  - **A deeper sense of self**

Fulfillment - Values

- **We are fulfilled when we orient around our values**
  - **Authentic and sustainable**

A need is something you must have in your life to function well. Needs drive our behavior - whether we are aware of it or not. If we are not conscious of our needs, we may be driven to behavior that isn't in our best interests. When our needs are not met consciously, our relationships with people are heavier and less joyful, because at some level we tend to become resentful when our needs are ignored. When a need is met, we feel good, satisfied, at ease, less anxious or threatened.

When your needs are *well* met, it is easier to orient your life around your values. Values are standards and principles you are naturally drawn toward. Values **add** to life; needs are required to function well.

And when a value is expressed, we feel deeply fulfilled. Values draw us, without urgency or effort, toward fulfillment. Fulfillment comes from expressing yourself fully and feeling the impact it has on others and yourself. It is the inner reward for being authentic - ***living YOUR life!***

Happiness <<<<< Satisfaction <<<<< Fulfillment

Take some time to explore these distinctions in your own life. You can use your journal to work through the suggestions and questions below. Taking time to do this will help you know yourself better. This, in turn, will help you upgrade your ability to make sound decisions in all areas of your life, from finance to relationships.

Happiness:

- You feel gratitude and want to bring more of this into your life. Begin keeping a gratitude journal.
- Define and do the things you love to do - list 10 of them.

- Look for more things to bring pleasure and joy into your life.
- Contribute to others, groups, and organizations.
- Listen to your own language; how many times a day do you say, "I should?"
- Write a list of 10 things you are merely tolerating - clear these up.
- What is something selfish that you could do for yourself today?
- Start a new project, doing something you love.
- Begin paying attention to what you want - to what grabs your attention.

Satisfaction:

- Expand gratitude by becoming aware of the abundance that is in your life - write out your abundance list - do small things to feel abundance in your life.
- Stop yourself from complaining - what is it that you can do if there's something that is upsetting you? If there's something you're frustrated with?
- Clear up your weekly and monthly budget - cover your highest priority costs and bills.
- Start a slush fund - even if its $10 a week.
- Establish boundaries for yourself.
- Eat nutritiously, exercise, etc.
- Stop the self blame - every time you go to beat yourself up have a positive affirmation ready to counteract this.
- Fix or eliminate the things you are dissatisfied with.
- Do the things you enjoy, or begin to move away from the things you do not enjoy.
- Ask yourself: "What do I need more of for me to live and function at the level I desire?"

Fulfillment:

- Begin to create things - a project, art, crafts, house redecorating, etc.
- Identify what brings you pride, a deep sense of pleasure.
- Enjoy a full day without making decisions about your future or life in general.
- Set a standard of excellence - do complete and full work.
- Create a large project - begin to think about leaving a legacy.
- Do what comes naturally to you.
- Master something - a new skill, hobby, etc.
- Honor your inner feelings, express yourself fully.
- Hang out with like-minded people.
- Ask yourself: "What qualities do I most admire in myself?"

Counteracting Self-Blame

Regret is a great waste of energy. Replacing blame with a proactive approach to improving your situation is an important skill in recognizing and satisfying your needs.

Affirmation

I will keep my words positive, because my words become my actions.
I will keep my actions positive, because my actions become my values.
I will keep my values positive, because my values become my destiny!

Application

Clarify what you need by paying attention to and writing down your negative thoughts. Next to them, write down a positive statement that counters this negativity poisoning your confidence. For example:

Negative Thought

"Boy, I really blew that job interview. I'm never going to find a job."

Positive Statement

"Well, I learned that I need to find a more intelligent way of answering that question. Next time, I'll do a lot better."

Outcome

Make the second statement realistic, incorporate a lesson learned, determine to take action and focus on a positive future outcome.

Identifying Values: the first step.

Values are simply things that matter deeply to you. We often hear this word used to describe morals or ethics. These are cultural values. This is not what we are referring to here. We are describing things that are deep within you, the things that make you unique - who you truly are. By expressing these things, you are being authentic, or true to yourself. In this way there is no right or wrong, no judgment (as we often experience with cultural values). There is no group consciousness about what the right values are, no one is determining them for you. This is very individual, specific only to you. Even if we have similar values to someone else, we will express them differently, coming from our inner authentic self.

Benefits of Being Values-Based and Therefore Authenticity-Based

- **Goal setting is easier and goals are reached more quickly.**
- **Your life purpose/vision comes to you more clearly.**
- **Fewer distractions occur; life is simple, but rich.**
- **You will be able to motivate yourself naturally.**
- **You will spend less money on things you don't need.**

Would it be a big change in your life to discover your inner values? We can take this a step further, and having discovered the things that matter at a deep level we can then begin to set goals and aspirations around these values. This process will simplify your life and focus your energies. It will help you choose things more wisely in your life - things that are a better fit for you.

Mary Jane was happy.
She had a great job, wonderful friends, and lived in a wonderful part of town. Yet most mornings she woke up asking herself why she was always doing the same "stuff." She was living proof that her goal setting had rewarded her with great "stuff" in her life, yet she had the sinking feeling that she was not living a purpose-driven life. She felt that many things were missing, yet couldn't put her finger on what they were! She didn't feel like simply setting goals for a bigger house, more money, or new trinkets. It was time to dig deep and find out what would fulfill her.

Working with a personal coach she began to ask herself what her needs, wants and likes were in life. This was tough - she didn't really know the difference. Through months of work, she began to realize that she had been feeling happy because she had created a lot of *likes* and nice things in her life. Yet her sense of not being fulfilled was because she only had a few *wants* happening in her life, and now she was realizing that she was not fulfilling her *needs*. She had needs that she had never even realized! By addressing her values, the things that mattered most to her in life, she began to reorganize her thoughts and create new goals.

Her new goals tended to focus on creativity and ingenuity. She enjoyed new things, new projects and interests. By exploring these, she found that she actually still created more money at work, as well as attracting more nice things into her life. It was just that she was doing things she loved, that were based on her values, and she was naturally attracting the likes along the way!

Key points in focusing on your values:

1) Your values are worth discovering.
2) Values are a deep and sustainable basis for goal-setting.
3) You are your values, your dreams and aspirations.
4) Values bring fulfillment, wants bring gratification (and often an emptiness.)
5) Values are an appreciating asset - being aligned with them gives you increased energy.

To make discovering your values easier we have included a list of some values. Read through this list and pay attention to those values that resonate best with you. You may have values that are not included here. By all means add them in. This list is not meant to be exhaustive; it is simply a tool to help you choose what you value most.

Adventure
Risk
Endeavor
Quest
Experiment

To Catalyze
To Impact
To Touch
To Coach
To Influence

To Create
Design
Invent
Synthesize
Imagination
Ingenuity
Originality
To Inspire

To Feel
To Experience

Beauty
Elegance
Attractiveness

To Contribute
To Serve
To Facilitate

To Discover
To Learn
To Observe

To Lead
To Inspire
To Influence
To Persuade
To Guide

Mastery
Expert
Excellence

To Relate
Be connected
Part of Community
Family
To Nurture
Be With

To Teach
Educate

To Win
Acquire
Attract

Pleasure
Fun
Be Entertained

Be Sensitive
To Touch
Perceive
Be Present
Show Compassion
Respond

Be Spiritual
Be Aware
Be Passionate

You are Your Values!

Values are that part of us that we are naturally inclined and drawn to, without effort or even goal setting. Values make up who we are, what we want out of life, and how we live. An example: some people are natural explorers - exploring at a different scale at 6 years old than at 40 years old. Exploration is a value to them, and if it is not part of their lives, then they will feel unfulfilled and dissatisfied.

Tom graduated at the top of his class at medical school, and went on to complete his residency in orthopedics. His high grades, his excellent surgical skills and his breezy bed side manner, allowed him to chose to work with the top team of surgeons in the city. This was a dedicated group, focused on long hours and tough cases. The work was challenging and exciting over the first few years. But because of the high pressure and fast pace, Tom began to feel burned out. He of course assumed it was because of the long hours. He focused on nutrition and exercise, determined to keep himself fit and strong. Yet he was still fatigued and worn out. A close friend began to ask him why, which had Tom begin to think long and hard about where his fatigue and burn out were coming from. He thought back to his years of school, and how he had worked longer and harder then to make it, yet felt vital and strong, with no signs of burn out. He realized that a pursuit of knowledge kept him feeling vital and young, enthused about his work, and overcame any potential fatigue from long hours and stress. He recalled a research position he had one summer that made him feel more excited about his work than he ever had since. Why had he stayed out of the research side of his profession? Well that was simple; you didn't make money doing it! And being a top student, and an excellent surgeon, he had naturally gravitated to the areas that would bring him the most income and outward success. Yet in this world, he had lost his enthusiasm and vitality. Was it worth it? Not any more! Over the next 6 months Tom began to restructure his schedule, and began to explore research avenues again. His success grew over the next few years, and he published ground-breaking research in the area of stem cells and immunology. True, he was making less money, but he was feeling more fulfilled, and therefore able to enjoy a rich and fulfilling life.

Being guided by one's values is an integral part of achieving success from the inside out. However, values are easily buried by challenges and problems in our lives. Whenever we are in survival mode, in fear, or sensing danger - our values naturally hide. Needs, shoulds and coulds, tolerations, incompletions, adrenaline, addictions, irresponsibility, stress, money, obligations and duties can all chase values underground. These things tend to dominate our lives, becoming the depreciating issues or assets on our balance sheet. They subtract and extract energy from us.

So, to begin uncovering your values you may first need to clear away some of the challenges that hide them from you. In the next chapter we will outline a couple of simple exercises to clear our tolerations, stress triggers, adrenaline issues, etc. The entire list will probably take working with a talented coach and/or financial planner, but we can help you quickly clear up some of the biggies. **Once you start to clear out some of the clutter of daily life, you can begin to sense and feel what your deep values are.** Then you'll be ready to set goals and focus on these values, making them your highest priorities.

The following are strategies to help you orient around your values:

- Adjust your priorities.
- Reset some of your goals.

- Focus on the area(s) that matter the most to you.
- May need to change jobs/occupation.
- Begin part-time work in an area you love, so you gain the skills to eventually move into this field.
- Stop tolerating things, putting up with things.
- Build a community of creative and like-minded people.
- Move to where you would love to live.

Traditional Goal Setting vs. the Coaching Approach

Here are three popular ways that we traditionally set goals:

1) *Consequence:* If I don't get A, then B will happen, which I don't want, so I want A.
2) *Fantasy:* If only I had X, then I'd be really happy.
3) *Should:* To be a success/good person, I really should set X as the goal.

The limitations or problems with this traditional approach are:

- We have to push ourselves.
- When we achieve the goal, it doesn't give us the long term satisfaction we really want.
- We spend our lives setting and reaching goals that we may not really want.
- The person becomes the goal, versus just working towards the goal.
- Going for the goal takes a personal toll on the goal-setter and his/her family/friends.

Coaching approach:

- Drop the goals you have been trying too hard for, for at least 90 days.
- Identify your top values, then set goals for each value.
- Set goals based on integrity.
- Eliminate tolerations, get needs met.
- Your coach will make huge requests of you, unreasonable at times, yet you will then launch out and dream and try new things.

This works because:

- The person begins to tell the truth about what they would really love, versus what everyone else wants.
- You begin to prioritize.
- You begin to have a sense of fulfillment.
- Goals are reached more quickly when you are accountable to a coach.

Aileen:

I know first-hand that values are powerful and progressive tools. As a financial planner, I asked myself how my work could support my values and allow me to become fulfilled without compromise. The vision for inspired wealth came when I embraced my desire to help others make a connection between their values, vision and resources. In this way my core values led me to become an innovator and facilitator of holistic approaches to finance that add value to others and contribute to our industry. Honoring my values helped me create a framework to do work that inspires and engages me fully.

How often do we adjust ourselves to fit into a situation instead of adjusting the environment to support ourselves? We strongly believe this has tremendous implications for all of our institutions. Most people accept that an institution is the way it is and adjust to fit the structure that is there, instead of recognizing that it doesn't serve their needs and values and taking some responsibility for creating a solution that supports them. We are all called to be leaders for change when we recognize that our environment is not supportive of our values. More people need to accept this call to leadership if we are to evolve the institutions in our society to serve our collective vision for the future. We need people to add value through values.

The Climber's Voice:

When I first began telling others that I wanted to climb a mountain, my voice wavered as I tried to convince people that this was a calling from a very deep place within me. As I spoke of my passion for this goal, I could see that they thought I was just plain crazy! At first this made me feel a bit lonely, but as I prepared for this goal and envisioned my success, I came to see that this was my path and that it was perfect for me, if not for anyone else. I had to listen to the voice within that told me that this goal would make the best use of my skills and teach me what I needed to learn. It would prepare me well for the rest of my life - I felt certain of that.

We each have the opportunity for personal greatness. Personal greatness comes from having a sense of completeness in our lives, which in turn comes from knowing that we have done the best we can with what we have... that we have been true to the best of ourselves. Dare to bravely follow your heart and to live your dreams with honor and integrity. Dare to live up to your potential.

"Like ability or a muscle, hearing your inner wisdom is strengthened by doing it."

— Robbie Gass

Learning to trust yourself and your own heart takes practice. So often we want concrete evidence before we act. We want to know that what we do is going to work, that it will be a success. But life doesn't work this way. You must therefore be your own guarantee of happiness. That is, no matter what happens, you must always believe in yourself and in your ability to make your dreams come true. The key is to keep acting in ways that *honor who you are*.

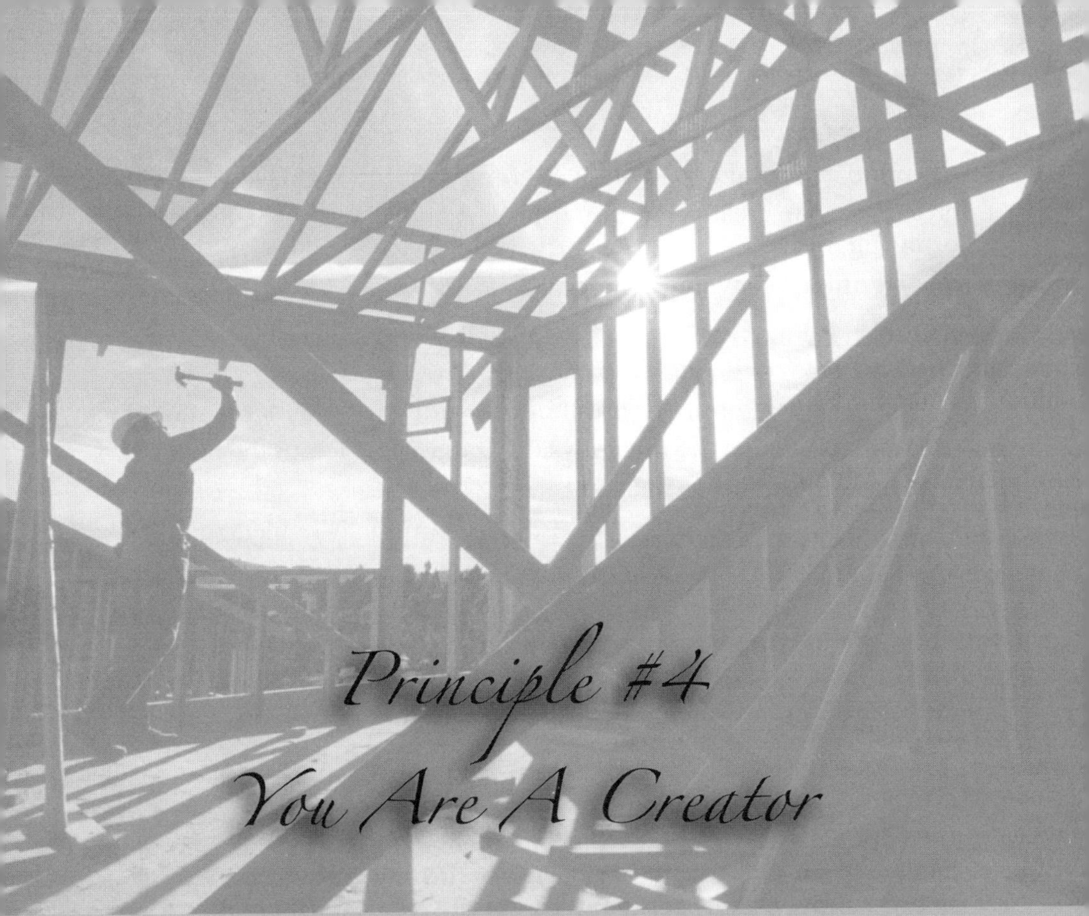

Principle #4
You Are A Creator

- ✓ All things are conceived in thought
- ✓ Creating vs. competing
- ✓ We are all here to manifest
- ✓ Create more value: attract more money

**"Life isn't about finding yourself.
Life is about creating yourself."**

— George Bernard Shaw

You really are a creator - every one of us is. In fact, fundamentally life and creation are really one and the same thing. You can't be alive without creating, so we believe it is vital to a satisfying full life to become conscious of what we are creating and the choices we make around that.

Your Mind Is a Generator

- Your mind can generate possibility through your thoughts at your will.
- You can learn to create your own solutions and added value, instead of borrowing from others.
- You determine how your brain thinks.

Everything Originates in Thought

- Think consciously, observe your thoughts and direct them intentionally.
- Manifesting is taking the metaphysical and turning it into the physical.
- We all have the ability to manifest.
- Authentic wealth creators know this: they continually hone their ability to create and add value.

Creating vs. Competing

One of the things you can learn, if you ever watch young athletes compete, is those who are constantly looking over their shoulders seldom win.

Aileen:
"When my daughter was involved in our community swim team I would volunteer my time to help with the meets and time the swimmers as they completed their races. It was incredible to see the athletes who were completely focused on their own skills get to the end of the race. You could pick them out from the others and watching them was pure joy! They looked oblivious to what was happening around them, their focus would not stray for a second from their goal. They knew that the very act of looking over their shoulder would cost them time and focus and ultimately this would cost them the race."

Professional athletes know the best way to win is to focus on your own gifts and set your standards from within. The same holds true for artists: they know their success depends of their ability to see the world through their own eyes and create in a unique way. They do not look at the creation of others and try to compete with it or imitate it. Like an athlete or an artist, the key to achieving your goals is to stay focused on your gifts and set your standards from within. You must design your own road map for success.

Sometimes what appears to be your Achilles' heel is really your gift to contribute. The truth is, most people who have become *successful* will tell you they had a tremendous challenge to overcome at the beginning of their journey. Each of us is different - this is a gift, not a challenge. In the final chapter of his best selling book, *The Millionaire Mind,* Thomas Stanley sums up the central theme in the lesson most millionaires have learned on their way to creating wealth: " It pays to be different." For many very successful people, the ability to "over-respond" to the difficulties in their lives has been the key to their success. When you think of yourself as a creator you'll be grateful for your uniqueness. You'll thank the heavens and see unique ideas as gifts and opportunities.

Hear Your Calling to be a Creator:

"A wonderful realization will be the day you realize that you are unique in all the world. There is nothing that is an accident. You are a special combination for a purpose and don't let them tell you otherwise, even if they tell you that purpose is an illusion. (Live an illusion if you have to). You are that combination so that you can do what is essential for you to do. Don't ever believe that you have nothing to contribute. The world is an incredible unfulfilled tapestry. And only you can fulfill that tiny space that is yours."

— Leo Buscaglia, Lecturer and Author

It is your birthright and ultimately your responsibility as a thread of the world's tapestry to be as brilliant in color as your creator envisioned. Know that you were not created in the image of mediocrity. You were made in the image of the creator and in you lies the ability to create what you desire. Just as nothing is an accident, your desires too are intentional. They are the unique color that can never be duplicated the tapestry needs if it is to achieve its brilliance. Denying yourself an opportunity to be everything you have imagined is cheating yourself of immeasurable joy that comes from fulfilling your authenticity.

Never satisfying that yearning for your authentic calling is robbing the universe of what it needs to thrive, and perhaps even ultimately to evolve and survive.

This requires that each of us, individually, understand the importance of living with a vision of our authentic desires and that we use our resources intentionally to move toward that vision. These desires collectively are what our future is made from, and our effort to manifest them is the energy of evolution. This energy is made from faith. Our belief, as we write this book, is that we are all destined for something greater than we might know, something greater than we know how to imagine.

Money and Evolution

Why do we use this discussion of money to help people understand the importance of authenticity and evolution?

Because people have a deep desire to create wealth, just as life has a need to advance itself. What most people often glance at, but fail to really see, is that creating lasting wealth requires much more than having and doing, it requires growing and evolving.

"Don't ask yourself what the world needs; ask yourself what makes you come alive. And then go and do that. Because what the world needs is people who have come alive."

— Harold Whitman

Finding Your Personal Vision

"Where there is no vision, the people perish."

— Proverbs

Discovering your unique powers as a creator requires adopting a compelling personal vision. Your vision is something that is a huge stretch for you, way out there beyond what your mind knows you can realistically do or achieve today or tomorrow. It's about what connects you to everything else. Many people get a quick glimpse of their vision at some point in their lives, and quickly shut it down. The brain immediately comes up with all the reasons you can't do this: it's unrealistic; you don't have time; what will people say; etc.

Instead of allowing this negative approach to entrap you, why not simply paint a picture and let it float into your consciousness - invite your vision into your mind's eye without evaluating or judging it in practical terms, remaining detached from its outcome. Allow it to be with you. Enjoy the excitement, the inspiration of your life's dream. Then you can begin to set your direction, your compass, toward it. You might not really see the entire picture all the time, but you will begin to sense it and learn to return to it for inspiration, knowing it is drawing you onward. You will discover that when you align your thoughts fearlessly to your life's purpose, you become a powerful creative force. Think of Nelson Mandela and his vision for his people. Lech Walesa and the Solidarity movement he led made an enormous impact on the chain of events that brought down the Berlin Wall. Would their achievements have been possible without vision and a strong sense of authentic purpose?

Take a moment to really think about the way your life could be if you were living your authentic purpose. In your journal ask yourself:

If I only made money from one thing, what would it be?
Is this what I am doing now?
What would I have to change to make this happen?
If I got all my joy from one thing, what would it be?
Do I feel a sense of peace and freedom?
What do I envision when I think of the life that I desire?

Spend some time here, allow yourself to fall in love with this vision.

- How at ease are you?
- How does it feel to be expanded this way?
- How do you feel about your relationships?
- How do you feel about your financial situation in your vision?
- What changes do you need to make so that you could afford to feel this way?
- What do you have to build?
- What do you have to take care of?

- What do you need to let go of to live this way? What dependencies? What assumptions? What fears?

Listen for the answers to these questions from within. Use your resources and focus your energy to transform this into what is real for your life.

Remember that you are trying to paint a picture. It is very important to be committed to your truth, **not your outcome**. Having a vision brings you the gift of focus. If you have a direction and you focus on implementing the habits that will get you there, then you are sure to achieve your dreams. While you work on your vision, don't fall into the trap of believing that you will be happy when you achieve everything. Instead, be happy in order to achieve the vision. Enjoy the process, the ride! **It is your LIFE!**

The Importance of Focusing on the Right Thing

Visualization is an essential tool to help you create the life you desire. Add focus to this, and you have a truly powerful combination. You've probably noticed that what you focus on is what you get more of. Here's what we mean:

Pretend you are mountain biking along a hilly single-track trail. You are speeding down this dirt trail carrying a lot of speed into the sharp turn at the bottom. The ground is loose. There are trees tight on either side...your adrenaline is pumping. Now stop for one second. Where is your focus? If it is on the trail ahead - good choice, you are safe. That is where you'll go. Focus on the trees and...as much as you don't want to go there...strangely enough you are pulled into the trees.

It is the same in life. Your ability to visualize and focus has a powerful effect on your outcome. Visualize and focus to see your goals and dreams clearly and include as much detail as possible. To help build these skills begin writing. A journal or diary will help you get in the habit of writing down your dreams. These seeds planted in your subconscious will bear fruit later on. You will be pulled in their direction on your life's path.

Push vs. Pull

It is amazing the difference that vision can make in our lives. Without the big picture, we spend our time and energy pushing in the direction of our goals, and we struggle on the treadmill of life. The difference in knowing and opening up to our vision is that we begin to feel drawn in that direction. We can't necessarily explain why we feel compelled to make certain choices or decisions, yet we know that we are being drawn into something. This is when synchronicities begin to happen in our lives - we meet people along the path who compel and support us in our new direction; we find and discover new resources, places and things at just the right time and place on our journey.

"In your lifetime the most sacred space you will ever need to create is the space within yourself — the place deep within your soul where you go to find peace and serenity and to connect with your true self. It's the quiet place inside where you return over and over again that keeps your thoughts sacred, your heart protected and your dreams alive."

— Nancy SantoPietro, Author of "Feng Shui: Harmony By Design"

"There are some people who live in a dream world, and there are some who face reality; and then there are those who turn one into the other."

— Douglas Everett

BIG IDEAS GROW They attract opportunities and things into our lives that we may not have expected or predicted.

However, this is tough when we are not feeling balanced, when we question our own self worth, when we are frustrated...then anything unrealistic will simply feel ridiculous or impossible. So let's not do our dreaming and planning on these days. These are the days for reminding ourselves of existing goals, not for setting new directions. Let's recognize these feelings for what they are: **when we are feeling unsupported in our dreams we most likely need to look at strengthening our foundation so that we can afford to think big.**

During these days revisit your Inspired Balance Sheet and look at your complete assets and liabilities. Go over you financial plan to remind yourself that you have created a strategy to strengthen your weak spots. Financial planning is an environment that will support you in feeling stronger and more able to shoulder your dream.

Got a big dream? You'll need a strong foundation.

Be careful of what you water your dreams with. Water them with worry and fear and you will produce weeds that choke the life from your dream. Water them with optimism and solutions and you will cultivate success. Always be on the lookout for ways to turn a problem into an opportunity for success. Always be on the lookout for ways to nurture your dream.

"Goals are a preview of future events and experiences in your life."

— Mark Victor Hansen

The Role of Power In Creating

Do you feel powerful over your life?

- If not, whom have you given your personal power to?
- Who is running your life and how?
- What percent of your life is your own?

Are you waiting for things to change so you will live the life you want?

We believe:

- You and only you are responsible for the life you have. You and only you can change your life. You do have the power to make those changes, but you have to take action.
- You have created the life you have today, and only you will determine the life you will have tomorrow.

"I have made myself what I am."

— Tecumseh

"In the long run, we shape our lives and we shape ourselves. The process never ends until we die, and the choices that we make are ultimately our responsibility."

— Eleanor Roosevelt

We are solely responsible for changing ourselves. If we really needed the cooperation of a spouse, parent, child, teacher, student, or boss in order to feel better, most of us would be trapped. The fact is, we create our own reality.

This is difficult for most of us to swallow. Although we may not be able to control everything that happens to us, we control its impact on our quality of life. As one famous NFL running back once said, "The day you take complete responsibility for yourself, the day you stop making excuses...is the day you start to the top." Most people who seem to be living the life of their dreams have at some point been manipulated, swindled, laughed at, abused, sued, and stolen from. Successful people see these injustices as temporary detours toward their goals or part of the success journey itself, not as reasons to give up.

Exercising Personal Power Means Taking Action

Now it is time to begin taking action on your vision quest. You have just deliberately formed a vision that appears to far exceed your current capacity to achieve it. What do you do now?

Apply the principle of Kaizen - take single, simple steps linking your daily actions to your overall vision.

Principle of Kaizen:

Create a Life Plan from Vision

Strategies

Projects

Tactics

The principle of Kaizen is gradual, continuous improvement instead of massive transformation, which tends to create fear and resistance. Take whatever step is the next most logical, even if it may seem trivial. This is the opposite of transformational change - taking change in huge leaps. An example of this is apparent when we want to make major health changes in our lives. We begin by running 30 minutes or taking a one-hour exercise class. The principle of Kaizen is to get up each day and do one jumping jack. In doing this every day, what happens is that one day you find you have done two. Two becomes four...and you create the habit of exercise in your life. In 5 years you see that you have created a pattern of exercise. You are healthier than those who began with huge transformational changes and quit from injury or non-commitment.

Kaizen means taking a step outside your normal limits - not a great leap, just a step - saying something you would normally keep bottled up inside, taking two more steps up a ladder if you are afraid of heights, and telling yourself you could do something you would have normally said you could not do.

Taking Action: from Goal to Project

Do you remember doing a school project that completely absorbed you? Treat this the same way. When you talk to others about what you are doing, refer to it as your current project. It has a more believable ring; you are simply working on a project. You have already said yes and are making room for it in your life. For example, instead of saying, "I need this time to think about my goal to learn to scuba dive," say, "I've set aside this time to work on a project that is important to me."

Chunk down your goals: 1-year, 3-year, 5-year plans - chunk goals until you have something you can take action on TODAY.

Here are some strategies for taking action:

- Make the time, and create the space in your life to think and do things that are aligned with your project. For example, if you always wanted to become an artist, a painter, take time to visit art galleries. Learn about other artists. Take a course. Visit an art shop. Make a list of the supplies you might need to start and what they cost. Start buying them a little at a time. Get yourself used to the idea of being a painter, let the excitement build in your heart. Have visions of yourself painting your truth.

- Shut off the television. The time that we allow to trickle out of our lives watching TV is enough time to accomplish many, many projects.

- You have more time than you think. If you stay focused on your project, you will learn to spend many small "Time Bytes" in a day focused on your goals. You will become inspired, act on your inspiration as much as possible. For example, if you love the work of an artist whose pieces you've seen at a gallery, and you find he has a web site or e-mail address, e-mail the artist, express your interest in his work. Ask for advice he may have for someone starting out. Where could you go to learn some basic skills? Most people love it when others take an interest in their work. Let your childlike curiosity and excitement take over. Go with your excitement.

- Determine what steps need to be taken to get to the life of your dreams. By now you have taken a look at the truth about your life. You've looked at how you are with money and you've looked at what you really, really want. Now you need to look at how to get out of your own way. For example if you are an impulsive spender, how are you going to avoid impulsive spending from today on? If you tend to over-commit, how are you going to ensure that every commitment you make is aligned with your vision?

- **CHOICE**. Where we are is based on the choices we have made. Our choices have determined the things that we attract to us - people, places, things and opportunities. You need to know that doing nothing different than what you are doing now is a choice. Even procrastinating is a choice. These simple ways of avoidance are not putting off choice; they are simply showing that your choice is not to change. Often we put off making a decision because we live in the black and white world of thinking we have to choose one thing or the other. If our choice is between A and B, we feel stuck. Let's blow this up to a bigger scale. Choice can actually be choosing A or B, it may be AB, or it might be neither. So in any one decision we have more opportunities than we initially recognize. An example - you are faced with the apparent choice to stay in your present job or quit. We generally make this decision based on our happiness or frustration levels. Why not begin to take the courses and training in something you would love to do? This might mean decreasing your hours, working part time, or altering some other factors around your job. By choosing bits of both, we are then working on the skill level of the new thing we would love to undertake, while still making some income from the previous work and not putting more stress into our lives. Leaving your job on the day you are the least happy will lead to financial, emotional and mental stress. This is no way to search for a new job, and a difficult position to be in if you anticipate a challenging learning curve in the new position.

Obviously many things come into play when discussing a basic topic like goals and objectives. The best way to approach realizing your goals is to break these concepts down into simple stages and steps, and begin to create a plan and strategy for you to utilize in your daily life.

The Climber's Voice

Whenever I spoke to people about my dream of climbing a mountain, the most frequent response came in the form of a question: "Where do you find the time?" Through creating this dream I have learned that taking the time to visualize my desire was the single most important factor in my achieving it. The moments that I allowed myself the space to be swept away by my vision were among the most free and productive moments of my life. These time-bytes seeded new possibilities for me, and as I dreamed of living my vision I developed the faith I needed to take a step toward it. Others might have thought I was resting, or escaping. When I think of this I can't help but smile: the truth is... I was creating."

"A clear vision, backed by definite plans, gives you a tremendous feeling of confidence and personal power."

— Brian Tracy

In the previous chapter we discussed the principle "Honor Who You Are:" this was about knowing your value and embracing your authenticity. The fourth principle, "You Are a Creator" is all about using your authentic calling to generate more *value*. We would love you to see that becoming a creator is about adding more value to life and how this eventually leads you to attracting more of what you want in your life, including personal fulfillment and financial rewards.

money = energy

Money energy flows to those who add value
Create more value...attract more money

Principle #5
Expand Who You BE, Not Only What You Have

- ✓ **All things are conceived in thought**
- ✓ **Building a life gives you energy**
- ✓ **Building a lifestyle is seductive and depletes energy**
- ✓ **Understand what sustains money vs. costs you money**

Climbing the Mountain Successfully Includes Coming Back Alive

The most successful mountain climbers, the ones who make it to the summit and survive, are those who understand that getting to the top is less than half the journey. Ensuring they have the physical and emotional reserves for the descent after what seems to be the climax of the expedition is the part many ambitious climbers miss, often to their great cost. The climb needs to be a balanced whole, just as a life needs to be a balanced whole. Endurance is essential for a safe journey.

Do I Truly Need This?

Are you building a lifestyle at the expense of your life? So often we catch ourselves about to buy something that an impulse tells us we don't need. After counting to ten, or taking a breath, ask yourself if this is something that is a true need. Or is this something that will momentarily stroke your ego or maintain a lifestyle.

So quickly we begin to create a lifestyle. We see what others have and want the same things. We visit friends who have just purchased the newest, the latest, the greatest, and we emotionally attach to getting this same thing. Keeping up with the Joneses - those other, apparently happier, more fulfilled people. Life seems more fulfilling when we can have these toys, these things. Yet, is it?

How many of us have switched to buying luxury products where we used to buy more ordinary things? Have you slowly been upgrading your tastes in all the things you consume? It's so easy to get caught up in this. If you have, and you find yourself working harder than ever before just to support your lifestyle, we encourage you to take this opportunity to think about the impact that this has had on your life. While it's true that we're all searching for a better experience in life, does upgrading your tastes in serviettes and soap provide us with a better quality of life? Does this add more energy to your life? Any idea what this might be costing you?

Is the stuff in your life moving you toward your highest goals or is it actually getting in the way and draining your energy? If you are concerned about your finances, or if you're too exhausted from working for the things you have to even enjoy them, then perhaps you are living a lifestyle at the expense of your life.

One of the most common characteristics of successful wealth creators (people who have been able to sustain their wealth) is that they focus their energy on how to increase their contribution, not their consumption. Legendary investor Warren Buffett is a great example. He is one of the richest men in the world, yet he still lives in the same house he bought three decades ago for $31,500 and drives an older Lincoln Towncar. Serious wealth creators, like Buffett, understand that becoming more, and contributing more, is infinitely more fulfilling than having more. And really, isn't that what we're looking for - not merely experiences, but more fulfilling experiences.

Has Spending Become an Emotional Reflex for You?

How about on bad days, when the going is tough? Too often it feels good to reward ourselves, or pick up our mood, with a purchase. When things are not working out the way we want, we sometimes tend to search for a sense of completeness and wholeness. This sets us up for a life of chasing and searching for what we feel is missing in our lives. We look for ourselves in all the wrong places. The result is that we don't find ourselves - then we feel even less complete, so we search in another external direction, only to come up disappointed again. This can become a viscous loop. The only way out of this is to recognize that you are already complete. Focus internally, not externally, for your identity.

Liza is a good example of this kind of behavior.
Liza and her husband were in their mid-forties. They had two children, both had high paying jobs and together they had created a comfortable lifestyle. Unfortunately, in the pursuit of building a lifestyle, they didn't realize how important it was to build a life together. As a result their marriage was strained: they were separated and were preparing for divorce when Liza came to my office. She was worried about how she would manage her finances and wanted to begin learning how to better take care of herself financially. Her primary concern was her spending habit. Liza had a difficult time controlling her spending: she was very attached to the lifestyle she and her husband had created. She felt she worked hard and deserved it. Liza realized that she had come to identify who she was with her lifestyle. Whenever she felt down she would shop to make herself feel better (more in tune with the image she wanted to portray). It took some number-crunching to show Liza what her lifestyle was costing her, and then it took some coaching for Liza to see that she was not her lifestyle. It turned out that Liza's lifestyle was not what she really wanted after all. In the end what she really desired was a sense of peace and completeness, or being in balance and in tune with her life. What Liza eventually learned is that she already had this, but was so consumed by her lifestyle that she didn't have time to discover her life.

Have you created a lifestyle for yourself?

Is it real?

Are you strengthened or weekend by it?

Does it reflect things that truly matter to you?

Does it support the way you want to be and achieve what matters most to you?

We have it backwards....

Here's how we think.		**Here's how we should think.**
HAVE		**BE**
DO	**vs.**	**DO**
BE		**HAVE**

We seem to think we need to *have* so that we can *do* in order to *be*. Instead it's much more effective to focus on who we *are* so we know what we need to *do* to *have* peace of mind and fulfillment.

Take a moment, close your eyes and think about the life you desire. What images are coming to your mind? The first thing that tends to come up for many is a picture of what you'd like to have. You may see the house of your dreams, a shiny car in the driveway, beautiful landscaping. This is actually a lifestyle. It would likely take some effort to get past that initial picture and drill down to your actual life.

Notice how easily we confuse who we are with what we have. Most people would love to have more money and live the life they desire, but few people see the path to this as clarifying and focusing on **who they Be** and getting that right first. Instead, some focus on what they *do*, getting their sense of identity from their roles as professionals, employees, or mothers. Most tend to put the cart before the horse and focus on what they *have*. This is not the way to build enduring wealth. It's backwards!

Please understand - we are not against living luxuriously. By all means enjoy the things you have. Become selective about what you have and make certain you can afford it easily. Your lifestyle should bring you energy and a sense of self-sustaining joy, not anxiety, exhaustion and entrapment. Focusing primarily on what you have creates all sorts of problems. You may not see them immediately, but eventually they surface, just as they did for Liza.

What happens when we focus primarily on *doing* or *having*? We identify and align ourselves with our roles, our money and our things. We become servants to these roles and these things instead of them serving us. This is a trap that many of us fall into when we pursue things and images of wealth (otherwise, appropriately named "trappings") for reasons that are external to us (like how we appear to others) without any meaningful connectedness to Self and our sense of being.

Here's an example:

You decide you want to buy a business. Did you make this decision based on your desire to express your entrepreneurial spirit, that is part of the truth of who you are. Or did you make this decision because you want to call your own shots and be seen by others as "a mover and shaker." The first reason is sustainable. It comes from a sense of who you are and expands this - it's the fulfillment of your being. The second reason has to do with wanting to appear a certain way to others. This is not sustainable. In this case becoming a business owner means setting yourself up to expand your need to live up to an image you created for yourself. Ironically, because you bought the business for the wrong reasons (based on something other than your essential nature) you might struggle in business. You may still feel compelled to live up to your need to portray the image of a "mover and shaker." This scenario can get you into lots of painful trouble! Unfortunately, it's very common.

Whether you are an entrepreneur, or an administrator, a teacher or a healer, an engineer or an artist - this is something that is a part of who you are, it's not something you can buy. Right choices are based on supporting who you are, not on what you have or wish to have, or who you would like others to think you are.

What we want you to see is that your success in all areas of your life is more sustainable when you realize that you don't need anything external to you to be complete. You are already complete. Sustainable progress will come to you when you focus on your pure essential nature, and honor your Self by aligning your resources with your being.

In today's society many look to *doing* and *having* for their sense of identity. The result is often creating a lifestyle, which often leads to despair and frustration, sometimes illness and dis-ease.

It turns out that *having* and *doing* isn't the freedom most of us are looking for. In fact, it can be very expensive. It's like putting the wrong fuel in your car: it will start and run, but eventually you'll sabotage the engine!

"What lies behind us and what lies before us are tiny matters compared to what lies within us."

— Ralph Waldo Emerson

Trust the Leading Indicators of Your Life

Attention is energy. What you focus on expands. When you focus on your authentic desires and interests, you feed them and they grow. Have you ever wondered what you might accomplish if you would take your desires and talents, hunches and interests seriously, if you would apply more energy toward them, make them the leading indicators of your life. Sometimes we just don't take ourselves seriously enough. We may love doing an activity, but never see it as an opportunity. Look to the things in your daily life that naturally interest you and explore whether there are opportunities and possibilities hidden in them that are just beyond your current thinking.

Trust that these talents and interests really are your leading indicators and they belong to you for a reason. All you need to do is learn to use them in a way that is meaningful for you. You can become innovative and create new roads for yourself to travel when you begin expanding your Self by applying energy and focus to what interests you most.

Attracting Career Advancement

Wouldn't you love to set up your life to attract instead of chasing, hoping and trying hard to make things happen? It is possible. To do this you need to pay special attention to your environment, your boundaries, your skills and your creativity. Think about this with respect to your career. Career advancement comes naturally to those who become too big for their current position. You can take action to attract a promotion by *expanding who you are* (mastering your skills) so that you outgrow your current position and attract a bigger opportunity. This is an integral part of personal finance that too often is completely ignored.

Aileen:
I was doing a call-in radio show about *Sudden Money* when a caller asked me how to best allocate the $5,000 her aunt had left her in her will. I asked the caller several questions and discovered that she was unemployed and hadn't any savings. I was very moved that the caller recognized this money as an opportunity to do something meaningful for herself, to elevate herself out of her current situation. Using the principle "Expand who you be, not only what you have," I asked her to consider applying the money toward an evening course to learn a new skill, which would make her more marketable and increase her confidence in applying for jobs. If she used the money to increase her income, this would provide her with an annuity-like return for the rest of her working years.

Most of us underestimate the opportunity even small amounts of money can present in our lives if we allocate them to expand our potential. See the opportunities of using your money to reveal your potential, not just to fill your life with stuff.

Expand Your Total Capital

As a rule of thumb pay particular attention to the liquid capital (financial reserves) and human capital on your balance sheet. In daily living take actions and decisions that will strengthen these assets and reduce the liabilities that are limiting your ability to respond to opportunities or challenges with confidence. To really strengthen your assets don't just think about investing more in things. Begin thinking about how you could invest more in your Self. What new skills could you build on that would enhance the talents you already have? How could you free up more time and money to apply toward developing the interests that you are most enthusiastic about?

Questions:

- What gives me energy?
- What drains my energy?
- What would I love more of in my life?
- What would I love less of in my life?

- What will it take to accomplish this?
- What will I have to clean up on the balance sheet that is draining me (things that I am putting up with, tolerating, or not dealing with?)
- What assets do I have that I can expand on?

Growth happens by evaluating our weaker areas, and working on those. We have been taught to ignore the weakness or weaker areas and to only focus on our strengths. Honor and utilize your strengths, yet recognize that growth and opportunity come from building and growing your weaker points!

Exercise: The resource builder

What three weaknesses do I have in the areas of work, play, and money? List three in each category.

Work	Rating	Play	Rating	Money	Rating
____	____	____	____	____	____
____	____	____	____	____	____
____	____	____	____	____	____

On a scale from -10 to +10 list where you would evaluate yourself in each of these areas (remember they are simply skills that you have not achieved excellence in because you have not been taught how or haven't focused on them yet).

- Which ones on your list stand out as being the greatest opportunity for growth (your lower scores).
- Now...who can mentor you, help you grow in this area?
- What programs or workshops can you take to learn these skills?

When you feel great about what you're doing, you will be more attractive to yourself and you'll be more likely to attract what you want. Confidence is attractive. There are so many books that proclaim the virtues of **THINKING BIG.** However, thinking big without a clear sense of being and a strong foundation can lead to frustration and fear. Thinking big and building a strong foundation will enable you to go confidently in the direction of your vision.

The Climber's Voice:

Climbing a mountain isn't exactly the kind of thing that someone calls you up and gives you the opportunity to do. It wasn't a matter of saying yes or no to someone else's idea - how long would I have had to wait for that opportunity

to come up? I needed to expand this idea by allocating energy and focus to it, and trusting that this would take me where I needed to be. That was the hard part. It was easy to dream about it, but I must admit the test came when I needed to put my money where my mouth was, knowing very well that doing so would mean giving up some of the creature comforts I had come to enjoy. The amazing thing was that once I began directing my resources to the climb, I started to believe in my ability to achieve it. The experience has been incredible and I wonder now who I might have become had I not made the decision to take the little voice inside me seriously. I can't imagine that I would have felt whole and complete, as I do today. I probably would have continued searching for something - but what? In the end, it likely would have been more expensive for me had I not followed my heart. I can't imagine what I would have had to buy to give me as much satisfaction as having fulfilled this dream. Now I feel satisfied and content, and I feel free to just live.

The Importance of a Strong Foundation

There's no substitute for a strong foundation. No matter how capable you are, if your foundation is not strong enough you will eventually need to go back and strengthen it before moving forward. Sometimes people know their foundation is not strong but they move forward anyway and ignore what they see. This usually doesn't work for long. Sooner of later something happens that makes us revisit our foundation and we finally see that to move forward we will have to strengthen who we are.

If you wish to improve your financial foundation, ask yourself, "Where am I spending more than I **need** to spend? How can I scale this down to support me instead of burden me. How can I use my money to create more energy and freedom for myself to move on with what's next for me instead of having it create more burden that keeps me stuck and drained of energy?"

Developing financial leadership is being intentional with money. Financial leadership skills enable you to use money to serve you and your values, and can prevent you from becoming a servant to your money. Commit to expanding who you are, by taking control of your finances and becoming more selective about the way you use money. Sometimes raising your standards about the things that you buy can be helpful. This may actually lead to more satisfaction from less stuff and a better quality of life.

Taking Action:

- Create a new rule that you will only buy things you absolutely love.
- Find joy in the little things in life, cut down the financial impact of splurges

and think of something you can buy for yourself for $10 - $15 that would feel like a luxurious treat. Indulge in that once in a while on a whim.

- Begin identifying the emotional costs that are associated with your success.
- Take small, significant steps this week to identify the things that truly matter to you. The rest is all just window-dressing. In a process much like spring-cleaning, it will be fun and likely refreshing to begin to shed some of this window-dressing, and strip down to the real you.

Proceed with a patient heart. When you understand that dry spells are merely speed bumps on the road to a great life, you'll begin to see them as gifts — a reminder to slow down so you can get your bearings, reevaluate your plans, and slowly shed the old you to make way for the new!

Expanding Ourselves Collectively: Evolution

The advancement of just one individual in society causes a series of advancements of varying degrees for all others in society. We are all connected.

You must be the change you want to see in the world.

— Mahatma Gandhi

Historically, affluence used to mean expanding yourself - pursuing education at the turn of the last 2 centuries. Today all too often affluence means escapism, inaction, insulation, stagnation - this has a huge impact on society. In 17th through 19th century Europe the wealthy didn't have to do menial work to provide for themselves. Their money afforded them the leisure and luxury of discovery and adventure. Kings would underwrite expeditions to look for new worlds, some of the greatest philosophers, artists and musicians of all time emerged in these eras and their legacies are still revered today. It was customary for the wealthy to study music and philosophy so they could contribute and entertain one another. This was all part of their social culture, and it fostered an expansion of ideas and talent that moved the world forward in significant ways.

Today the luxury of leisure time is more prevalent than ever, but how do we use it? Do our social endeavors today support our creativity and the evolution of humanity? Do we as a society encourage individual mastery? When we gather with friends, how do we entertain one another, what do we talk about? While it is easy to point out that life is much different today than in the 18th century, one of the factors that we believe will have serious consequences for our era is that with so many distractions it is very challenging to focus enough to achieve mastery. Who today would have the patience and the mastery to paint the Sistine Chapel?

Our culture has moved away from customs and activities that support creating. Much of our social activity is focused on escaping and being entertained. "Escape to the movies, escape to the beach or mountains, escape to the cottage

- just escape." We are often focused on moving away from things, but are we focused enough on moving toward anything? If what you focus on expands, what happens when we focus on escaping instead of creating? How will the things we are escaping ever change and evolve, how will we change and grow?

Bob's major goal was to have a speedboat. He spent many moments visualizing getting to the lake and enjoying the thrill of freedom and speed on the open water. He researched his purchase thoroughly and after many months of saving, he bought a boat. He was certain that this purchase would change his life, and it did. After several months the novelty had worn off, and Bob realized that the boat hadn't made him as happy as he thought it would. There was a lot of work and expense involved in owning the boat and somehow it wasn't as satisfying as he had imagined it would be. After some time Bob realized that it wasn't the boat that he had been dreaming of; he had been dreaming of getting away from his job, which he dreaded every Monday and wanted to escape from every weekend. He realized that the key to finding the joy he was looking for was not in escaping, but in changing his environment so he wouldn't feel the need to escape.

Consider this:

- Take a look at your toys. Do they facilitate creating or escaping?
- Take a look at how you spend your time, talents and treasure. Are you utilizing them to grow yourself, your family, and/or your community?

Creating a Legacy

So often we are caught up in what will happen today or tomorrow. Our decisions are often based on short-term problem solving or single-issue events in our lives. By getting caught up in the details (even though details are important), we often lose sight of long-term plans or visions. Yet, without long-range forecasting, how can we accurately determine if things that are being presented in the here-and-now are really right for us?

Our culture has such incredible focus on short-term gratification and short-term living in general. Long-range planning is usually 5 to 10 years. Is this really long range? Let's look at the Japanese culture. In many instances, decisions for families in Asian cultures are based on what effect they will have on their children's children - not for themselves, but for the entire future of their families. This is called creating a legacy.

This adds incredible impact to the choices we make today. Creating a legacy is an important element of the "Expand Who You Be, Not Only What You Have" principle. When trying to decide if a new job is appropriate, how about asking yourself questions that go beyond today - meaning, money and opportunity - and impact on the future? For example, will this enable me to express values that are important to me? Will this enable me to spend time with my children when they are young enough to want to be with me? Will this new role have impact on other people's lives?

How about the decisions that we make about our health? Choices of the foods we eat, the exercise we do, or the stretching program we implement. This will increase your energy and ability to partake in activities for the long term. It will add years to your life - longevity! Besides your own health, what message is it sending to the people around you, your kids and their friends?

What long-term impact will the decisions that you make today have? When we begin to think about creating a legacy for our family it shifts our perspective and opens up incredible dreams and opportunities for us. More important is the fact that when you establish the values and principles that are behind the legacy you choose to leave, you can then measure all daily items against this. Do they fit or not? This makes your daily choices much easier. This allows you to stay living in the moment - in the present - at the same time creating a legacy for yourself and your family.

Plan Your Legacy

Don't be so afraid of the end. Plan for this - it happens to us all. Make sure the choices you make today will fit in with the legacy you choose to leave behind. This is the ultimate in expanding who you BE!

Principle #6
Let Go and Eliminate

- ✓ **Let go of what no longer serves you, including goals that don't reflect your true values**
- ✓ **Eliminate the things you are tolerating that keep you stuck**

A perfectly-planned expedition sets out with exactly the right supplies and materials and exactly the right team members. Even for very experienced adventurers and mountain climbers, the perfect expedition has yet to be mounted. In real life, we constantly re-evaluate and make changes, and the most successful expeditions have managed to adjust and shed excess baggage and misfit team members as the need became obvious.

What do I need to let go of in order to welcome in the new life I desire?

If we keep doing what we have been doing, we'll keep getting what we've got! If we say we want different things and aspects to our lives, we must make changes from the path and course that we are currently on. The easiest way to do this is to clean up and clean out. An example of this is our closets - by cleaning them out, getting rid of all that we don't use anymore, this creates more room in our lives. With so much stuff in our lives, it is difficult to show any empty spaces or vacuums that we can fill with great new stuff. This is a basic energetic principle - to attract more, there has to be room to attract it to.

Money is the same. To attract more we must often make changes. And this doesn't always have to be waiting for a new job that pays us more. It can simply be cleaning up and cleaning out, just like the closets.

There are basically two approaches we can take:

1) Let go of things that are not serving us.
2) Eliminate things that are draining us.

Aspects of our lives that are not serving us still keep us busy and fully committed. There is then no room for new opportunities, new enterprises, or simply the vacuum that pulls things to us. If there are also things in our lives that are draining us, then no matter how much great stuff you try to bring into your life, there will always be things draining your resources. This ends up being like a leaky bucket - no matter how much water you keep putting in, if there are holes then the water simply drains right out.

With wealth and fulfillment the same principles hold. If you put more dollars into things that don't fuel you or things that drain you, then you are not adding value to your life.

Letting Go Frees Up Energy

- Let go of goals you've been pushing too hard for.
- Respond to change by becoming flexible and letting go of what no longer serves you.
- Let it go - forgive people and situations from your past. Learn the lessons, and move on. We expend incredible energy on old wounds and hurts. Either address these old situations head on, or simply let them go and move on.

Eliminate Energy Drains

Travel light by eliminating the following from your life:

- Friction
- Tolerations
- Expenses
- Obstacles
- Delays

Let go of goals you've been pushing too hard for. There may be a lesson in the ***Friction*** that occurs around that goal. Sometimes a goal can wear us down instead of inspire us. This occurs when goals are set from outside ourselves instead of from the inside. When goals are not set from our values they can be difficult to achieve and lead to frustration.

Eliminate ***Tolerations***. A toleration is anything we put up with that drains us of energy. It is anything that pulls us off focus or off track. For example, when you walk into your child's room and it is a disaster area, it pulls your attention and focus to that. You get frustrated, or in the other extreme, you ignore it. It takes energy to do something with our feelings. This is a toleration. We all have hundreds and in some cases thousands of things in our lives that we are tolerating. Beginning to clean up simple things that we are putting up with will begin to plug the energy leaks that are draining us.

Expenses in some form are a reality in all of our lives. We can have both direct or indirect expenses. Indirect expenses are like the hidden costs of things. We are suggesting that you begin to take stock of how much everything is costing you, including both the direct and indirect costs. That television or stereo system has the direct costs, yet it also has the indirect cost that comes from not investing the same amount of money, and over time reaping the investment capital from it. There is a much higher price tag to it than simply the price tag you see immediately - there are hidden opportunity costs of what that money could grow and become.

We may begin to see that specific things in our lives are costing us more than we are willing to pay. Dig deep and find things that may not look like they are costing you money, but they are costing you energy. And remember that energy really equals money. This might include organizations that you belong to, which take time and energy away from higher priority things in your life. It might be that the work you are doing is taking you away from your family more than you want it to. Look for specific examples in your own life. In your journal begin to calculate the amount of direct expenses in your life, and more importantly the indirect expenses. Be specific to address the action steps to clean up some of the expenses in both categories. Building wealth requires that you stop spending more than you have, in dollars, time and energy.

Obstacles and delays may be strong messages for you. Pay attention to them. Instead of continually trying to push through the road blocks or delays in your life, why not stop and assess whether you are headed in the right direction. Stop, look and listen. Take the time to stop and ask yourself some questions. Is this goal realistic - is it where I truly want to be headed. What hidden costs will occur if I keep pushing in this direction? Look at all the aspects of what you are doing by pushing and continuing to come up against obstacles. Are there ways to change your approach and still get to where you want to go? Ask for advice, listen to what others have to say, and more importantly listen to your own inner voice and intuition. Is it time to make changes?

Find like-minded people. Stop hanging out with people who drain you, with whom you don't share interests, or who gossip and talk about others. These are destructive habits. Find people who are interested in developing themselves, growing themselves, working on things that matter. You can grow and evolve together.

While it is certainly true that a period of apparent stagnation or inertia sometimes means we just need to have faith that we're on the right track, at other times it may mean something more. It may be that you need to loosen your grip or let go of something — an old habit, an outdated belief, or a strategy that doesn't serve you anymore.

Sometimes this letting go is more tangible. For example, you might need to end an unsupportive relationship to set the stage for becoming the new you. Or, you may need to let go of an unrealistic expectation.

Janice:
A friend who was beginning to focus on her personal foundation was working in the area of her self-love and her relationship with her body when she realized that she needed to give up the fantasy that her body would ever look like something out of a fashion magazine. Only then could she continue without sabotaging her success.

Detachment - Patience

Not needing a particular result immediately frees you. You will make the best progress if you are detached about the present moment, accepting it as it is without fighting it, getting frustrated and losing hope. Detaching from the future outcomes is even more difficult - learning this more patient approach to life is difficult when most of our upbringing has tied things we do to future outcomes. Most of us spend a large sum of time and energy doing things in the present with a specific future outcome in mind.

We see these same expectations with our money. Many times we will invest or spend dollars, expecting to see specific results. This is even more evident when you invest at a point that you may not actually have extra cash on hand to spend. You invest it with specific expectations to how much and when this will give you rewards. This is why we need to have a sufficient time-horizon in investing - to afford detachment and avoid judging at the wrong time. If we are at a point where we need the income from the investments, we will not be detached from the outcome. We will watch the investment, and often pull our dollars out at the wrong time.

Some Action Steps for Letting Go

In your journal write your ideas and comments in the following areas:

1) Who is really important to you and who is simply a minor character in your life? You can tell the difference because important people in your life add joy and energy. Spend time with these people, and avoid those who drain you.

2) Find three things in your life that are lifestyle choices and that you know are hindering you. How could you eliminate them within 30 days? Pay careful attention to what immediately comes to mind. Listen with your heart, not your head, and in your Inspired Wealth Journal write down the answers regardless of how strange or unexpected they may be. Once you have done this, sit with this information for awhile before taking action.

3) Forgiveness:
    - Forgive yourself
    - Forgive others

To begin this, write out some of the situations from your past that bring you pain, guilt or frustration. Write out the details that you continue to beat yourself up over. Are they accurate? Many times they are based on our perceptions at that time - more based on emotion than facts. What has come to light since that may help you see a different point of view. What will it take to simply let some of these experiences go? What did you learn from those events in your life?

Use this same approach with people in your life for whom you have hard feelings. What will it take to let this go? Can you simply write about the situation and the script that you would love to say to that person - then burn it, and let your emotions go at the same time.

Forgiveness will relieve you of more excess baggage than any other action you can take. Let go of guilt and regret for past mistakes. You accomplish nothing by feeling guilty. There are no mistakes, just lessons to be learned.

In all these things, remember the principle of Kaizen - small steps, taken consistently, will take you the farthest.

At high altitude, on Everest and other peaks over eight thousand meters high, climbers without supplemental oxygen sometimes progress at the rate of one step for every ten breaths. This is slow progress indeed, and if they give their attention to how far there is to go, their courage can fail them, their energy will drop. So they concentrate on the next step. Just the next step. And during the

rest-pauses to reoxygenate, they concentrate on the returning energy, and perhaps a landmark, a rock or feature of the snowfield they will reach in ten steps. No more than that. The summit does not exist, just the next step. Approaching a seemingly impossible task this way, Sharon Wood, who describes herself as an ordinary person, was able to become the first North American woman to climb Everest, and the first of all women to climb Everest by an untried route.

Principle #7 Be Willing to Climb Your Mountain

- ✓ **Often what we must do is not what comes easiest**
- ✓ **Climb the mountain path of your personal evolution**
- ✓ **Accept that it is not easy to stick to your plan with money... be willing to do it anyway**

Mountains and Money

If you are serious about your inspired wealth quest, you must be willing to climb your mountain. Mountains have long been symbolic of life's challenges and man's desire to overcome adversity and triumph. Being willing means that you are open to the adventure of your life and the unknown terrain ahead. It is simple common sense to look for guides who are mountain-climbers, who have tackled similar challenges and thrived.

You wouldn't embark on such a journey without preparing yourself by becoming aware of what you'll need and gathering those resources and reserves. Our journey to achieve our goals and fulfill our life's purpose also requires that we become aware of what we need to succeed. How do we need to augment our present skills? How much do we need in reserves to survive, and ultimately thrive. Climbing a mountain without all of this information would be significantly more dangerous. It is wiser to find the simplest way up the mountain.

Map out your journey before you begin. Developing a plan that will guide you is creating a structure for decision making on your journey. This helps you stay on course instead of reacting in fear and taking the wrong path if you become temporarily disorientated in your climb.

We Believe:

Sustainable wealth creation demands personal development, which is an evolutionary process that takes us forward and upward. If we continue on our wealth-creation journey using only the knowledge we began with, we would not be able to keep up with the changing world. As we change and evolve, it is imperative that our perspective and approach to managing our lives, our money, and our creation of wealth, also change.

The Challenge Of Sudden Wealth

The biggest difference between a self-made millionaire and a lottery winner is that the lottery winner didn't evolve to attract money. This creates a great sense of insecurity for the lottery winner. In some ways it is similar to when successful business owners give their children a business that they didn't help build. Their lack of money maturity makes it difficult for the recipients to sustain the windfall. This is because they don't have a solid personal reference point, acquired from making decisions that lead to favorable and sometimes unfavorable outcomes, to help them learn how to make good decisions with money. For this reason, on a smaller scale, we recommend that parents allow children to make spending decisions with their allowances, even if they clearly see those decisions as being mistakes. Actually while the children are young, parents should celebrate their children's mistakes with money and use these times as opportunities for important life lessons. A small $20 mistake can provide the same lesson to a young child that a $20,000 mistake teaches an adult. The amount of money is relative and the sooner the learning, the easier for the child... and the parents.

The analogy of climbing a mountain lends itself beautifully to illustrating the challenges of sudden money. Imagine you're climbing a mountain and you take every step carefully. You negotiate the tough spots and gratefully overcome them, learning from the challenge they presented. You sigh with relief when you come to the easy parts and see them as opportunities to get ahead. Sometimes there are what seem to be insurmountable challenges. At times, you may even have to move backwards before you can move ahead. Throughout your climb you are sustained by your desire to reach the top. You trust that the view from the top will be worth the struggle and you intuitively grasp that not climbing may be even more dangerous, because climbing is something you know you need to do.

On the other hand, how would you feel if someone took you on a helicopter ride and dropped you on the top of that mountain? You didn't choose to climb; you didn't have the deep desire to make it to the top of that mountain. But there you are, dizzy from the height. At first you are thrilled with the view, it's exhilarating and beautiful. But soon the novelty wears off and there you are on top of the mountain needing to make choices. You fear making the wrong choices: after all you didn't get up the mountain using your own skill. What happens if you fall off the mountain? How will you ever get back up? You don't have a map, you didn't bring a guide. Others are depending on you to make the right choices, but how do you make sense of it all in the midst of so much rapid change in your life? You know you need a map - the problem is the maps are sold at the bottom of the mountain. At the top everyone assumes you know the way.

Most of us don't win the lottery and perhaps we shouldn't be too envious of those who do. There is great value in choosing a path, getting a map and putting one foot in front of the other with consistency and resolve in the face of challenging terrain and distractions. In today's world of fast-paced change, the distractions are numerous and growing. Our time is increasingly fragmented as we all live busier lives. To overcome this, our commitment needs to be stronger than ever, our focus needs to be clearer and we need to make intentional use of all our energy.

Be Willing

To be willing is the ultimate expression of faith in yourself and in the benevolent nature of the universe. Whether you are willing or not will depend on whether or not you see the universe as a benevolent place that always guides you toward where you need to be.

- Are you truly willing to attain your goals?
- If you are willing, the obstacles, fears and doubts will have less power to block your efforts.
- Developing a financial plan is like mapping out your journey before you begin vs. going blindly into the unknown.

- Be willing to plan, be willing to see and look.
- Be willing to invest. We learn lessons better when they cost us time, money or energy. Invest yourself in the process of financial planning. It will reward you with new energy, both mentally and financially, to move you toward your vision.

- Be willing to accept the good with the bad along your journey. Accept that it is not going to be easy to do what you intend, but be willing to do it anyway. This speaks to a holistic understanding that all of your challenges and joys work together to help you evolve and grow.

People who are willing to climb their mountain are able to see the value added as well as the limitations of their choices.

They enjoy the focus, energy and momentum and do not feel cheated by having to give up other projects or activities in order to pursue their goals. Their perspective about what is important, and thus worth wanting, shifts. They extend their boundaries and prevent those who are critical of their goals from disrupting them and weakening their spirits.

Being willing to climb your mountain involves being willing to change your frame of reference from the pursuit of happiness (which is an elusive moving target) to the real prize: the pursuit of a fulfilling and rich life, which embraces all of life's experiences, the joys and the sorrows.

Sylvia had a deep desire to become a doctor. She was the mother of 2 children and her family finances didn't require that Sylvia work. At the time, she didn't understand why, but her intuition told her to pay attention to her desire to care for the sick. She felt this was her calling. With the support of her husband, Sylvia went back to school for several years and juggled her rolls as a mom, wife and student. These were very challenging years for Sylvia, and studying took over every spare moment she had. At times, she wondered where she was getting all the energy to balance her studies with her family life, but she had it, and she was using it to make her dream a reality, one exam at a time. Her friends couldn't understand why she would put herself through such challenges. They wondered why she chose such a hard road with two small children - clearly she didn't need the money. Their lack of understanding drove a rift between Sylvia and her friends, and although this saddened her, she accepted that this was a price she would have to pay to answer her call and live her life fully. In some respects, it would have been easier not to take her calling seriously and live the way others expected her to, but Sylvia knew that this would have been the ultimate sacrifice. To come to the end of her life and know in her heart that she hadn't answered her call, that she wasn't willing to live the life of the person she authentically was - this was not something Sylvia was willing to do.

Perhaps you are not prepared or willing to pay the price of achieving your dream. Can you estimate the cost of achieving your goals? Are the costs going to outweigh the gains? This is a question you need to consider. As we have shown with the Inspired Balance Sheet, there are often tradeoffs in getting what you want, and there is also, on the other hand, the cost of not having the life you desire. Denying yourself even the attempt to create what you desire can be the most expensive decision you ever make. There are heavy costs to not pursuing your dreams and aspirations. Write them down, and be very aware that they will continue to affect you for years to come. Somewhere in the middle there is a balance that requires many transitions and periods of imbalance followed by the enlightenment that brings us back to equilibrium.

Saying Yes

Being willing means looking holistically at all the pros and cons of a situation, the good and bad consequences, and saying yes to all of it. Knowing that the good stuff will bring you joy and the difficult stuff will evolve you to become more - more capable; more compassionate; more faithful; more grateful; more experienced; more wise; more of who you truly are. Saying Yes to all of this journey and recognizing the distractions along the way for what they really are, instead of what they appear to be, is an all-embracing experience of what it means to truly live. If you can say yes to all of it with enthusiasm and joy, and if you have prepared for the journey, then you're willing and ready to climb your mountain.

The Climber's Voice:

I knew that this journey would take much from me, but I was willing to experience the sacrifice in exchange for the promise of what I would gain by learning more about what it meant to truly be me, fulfilling my purpose.

Resist Looking Over Your Shoulder

To be a successful climber, you will also need to be willing to stop looking over your shoulder at how and what others are doing. Begin to focus not on how you are doing relative to others, **but how you are managing your own potential**. Take a look at your own circumstances, where you came from, and focus on where you want to go. Be willing to create your own standards from within and measure your results based on your own metrics, not the metrics of others with different paradigms on different paths pursuing different callings. Being willing to climb your mountain depends on your ability to reach within for all your inspiration to stretch and reach the top.

You will need to be willing to devote significant amounts of energy to simply staying focused on your goals. Be prepared to experience many tests along the way, which will make you question what you have chosen. You'll find lots of reasons to get off your path and stop climbing your mountain. Sometimes these will be obvious distractions, other times they will appear so logical that it will be hard for you to recognize them for what they are - **DISTRACTIONS**. You need to be willing to step over all of these and summon the courage to do what is necessary to continue the climb.

Let's take a look at how this applies to your investments. If you commit to a long time horizon in equities with the intention of being a successful investor, and the market is down for a couple of years in a row (and particularly if these years are at the beginning of your investment experience,) you may be distracted from your desire to fulfill your financial goals by looking only at the negative returns. Logically this doesn't feel like a distraction. It feels like reality. However, we know that over the last 50 years international equity markets have averaged more than 10 percent and getting through those difficult years is tough. But packing it in and getting off the path will mean that you won't be there to experience the good years that have historically made equities far more rewarding than any other asset class. In this recent bear market it takes great energy to simply focus on the plan and stay on the path. It requires that you put enough distance between your emotions and the challenges of the current environment to recognize distractions for what they are and to remember that within the challenges are also opportunities. Your success in investing and in life comes when you can see the whole of the matter, accept it, and be willing to develop a framework of thinking that carries you forward. Keep moving through the emotional extremes of excitement when things are going well and of fear when things are not.

"To invest successfully over a lifetime does not require a stratospheric IQ, unusual business insight or inside information. What's needed is a strong intellectual framework for decisions and the ability to keep emotions from corroding that framework."

— Warren Buffett

An Important Ingredient of Success

Being willing to develop a financial plan and the strong intellectual framework that will support you in executing your plan is an important part of your journey to success and sustainable wealth creation. Thomas J. Stanley, author of *The Millionaire Mind* and coauthor of *The Millionaire Next Door,* is a top authority on America's truly wealthy. Stanley's work shatters the vision we have of the wealthy as living the lifestyle of the rich and famous. Stanley conducted more than two decades of studies, looking at the lifestyle habits of true millionaires in the United States. His research paints a more realistic view of the wealthy. Stanley points out that wealth accumulators spend nearly twice the number of hours per month planning their investments as do those who have high incomes but end up accumulating little wealth. They have a budget and know what they spend on everything. The most satisfied wealthy people don't just have financial goals, they also have clarity about what they want in life and recognize that the path to success takes persistence and discipline, planning and sacrifice.

Having a strategy for how you will use your resources to move you toward your vision affords you a sense of confidence. Knowing that you have taken into account many of life's scenarios and what ifs to prepare yourself for your journey makes your footing more secure. Financial planning, at its core, is about making you stronger, so you can boldly go into your future.

When we understand the assumptions that we individually make as we plan for tomorrow, we become increasingly aware of the implication of what can happen if those assumptions turn out to be mistaken. In a world where change is imminent and constant, this type of financial intelligence is a survival skill. Welcome to an experience where emotional intelligence meets financial literacy and is facilitated through the coaching of a financial planner.

Financial planning guided in this way by a skilled practitioner who coaches you as you develop in the direction of your vision is an opportunity to strengthen your Self in all areas. The benefit is a much smaller chance that life will catch you completely by surprise and totally unprepared. This is the ultimate risk reduction strategy.

The Power of Financial Leadership

To climb the mountain successfully, you will need to be willing to exercise personal leadership. You will need to be willing to rely on your Self for the answers and be willing to trust that when you ask the right questions, you will find them.

You're willingness to look within and be satisfied that you are in the right place is critical. The greatest effort as you climb the mountain is in being willing to influence yourself in taking the next appropriate steps as you respond to the environment and the conditions on your route. If you are not willing to move forward in ways that align with who you truly are (instead of who others would like you to be) then you will become distracted and it is likely that you will not be successful in reaching your goals.

You will learn as a climber that you are solely responsible for staying on your path. Some may support you, others will distract you. You must accept this and step over it if you are to consistently take the right steps that will lead you to achieve your goals. You will need to be willing to prepare for the financial and life implications of your environment and hold on to your vision with faith and with purpose if you are to resist the distractions along the way. This is the essence of leadership. In applying this to finances, we call this financial leadership.

Since making appropriate decisions about money is a core skill for all of us in attaining success, financial leadership is required curriculum in the school of life. If we are not willing to develop leadership with respect to how we use our money energy, we will find it difficult to fulfill our true potential. If we are not using our money energy intentionally to create the lives we desire, we are most likely not using our many other forms of energy with intention either. So be willing to take seriously how you use money. Be willing to develop your own intellectual framework for making money decisions in your life. The 12 principles will guide you and provide a framework for connecting to your money in a positive and multidimensional way. As you move forward and upward on your journey you can use these principles to help you tap into the value within and create true wealth and lasting success in your life.

Advertisers bombard us with many distractions as they try to convince us about what we need to be happy. Many of us listen to their advice. We think to ourselves, "Oh, is that what I'm missing? I should get one of those, then I'll have more joy in my life." In this unintentional way, we get caught up in a vision of lifestyle that keeps us busy enough to ignore our need for deeper fulfillment. There are many things that support the pursuit of our dreams by freeing up time, giving more energy, and generally making us stronger. There are many more things that appear to do this, but instead use up our time, drain us of our energy, and simply distract our attention. Being willing to climb your mountain will mean that you will need to exercise leadership to look past these distracting drains on your energy and take a more proactive approach. You will need to concentrate your energy on your purpose and in the direction of your dreams, because if you begin to diffuse your energy too much, you risk eroding your power to continue the climb.

"Look at your past. Your past has determined where you are at this moment. What you do today will determine where you are tomorrow. Are you moving forward or standing still?"

— Tom Hopkins

Are you truly willing, committed, to attain your highest goals? If not, they may not be the best expression of your values. Something that is of great value to you is unmistakable. You will pay whatever price is required to keep moving in the direction of your true values. An example: your career - if you are on course and engaged in career choices that you love, you will step up and move, even to a new country, to pursue your dreams and aspirations in your chosen field. If you are simply doing a job and it calls for you to relocate, you will either feel resistance and therefore face great challenges, or in many cases you simply will not go - meaning that you are not willing to pay the price.

Truly committed individuals are passionate about their goals, so much so that others are intrigued by or attracted to this passion. It inspires and energizes people.

Are you willing and open to evolving in a way that makes attaining your goals easier? Doing the type of inner work and personal development that we believe is imperative in this process will make your goal setting revolve around your inner values and dreams. This will bring a different energy to your goals, an attractive energy, a more authentic energy. And this attraction will draw and pull the things you are aspiring to create more easily into your life.

Are you willing to make the changes required to manifest your desire?

You need to truthfully answer this question. All the coaches, financial planners and self-help books in the world will not help you if you are not willing to take the actions that you know in your heart will create the life you desire. If you are willing, the obstacles, fears and doubts will have less power to block your efforts.

If you do not really want change, stop paying it lip service, and, for goodness sake, stop wasting your money on self-help books!

If you really, truly want the life you desire, then know that **change is inevitable**. You cannot get a different result if you keep doing the same thing. It may not be easy, but you could be surprised. Making changes that appear difficult at first can produce results that make other things easier. The universe has a way of balancing.

The artist is nothing without the gift, but the gift is nothing without work.

— Emile Zola

There are times when we say we want a goal and feel we can achieve it, but lack the deep desire to make the necessary changes. If this is your experience we recommend that you ask yourself how **not** getting the goal may be serving you. For example, perhaps not making the required changes that could lead to attaining your goal is giving you the ability to blame others or your circumstances for your unhappiness and lack of success.

When working with professionals who would like to increase their fees, but have a difficult time doing so, it often comes to light that the reason for their reluctance to increase fees stems from their unwillingness to commit to providing a higher level of service in exchange. If they charge less than they're worth they get to hold onto the excuse that because the client is getting a bargain on their fees they don't have as much responsibility for the quality of the service they provide and can justify cutting corners.

In this way, our reluctance to commit ourselves and be willing to be our personal best, shines through in our relationship with money. We know that more money means more commitment, more responsibility and many people are not willing to pay this price. But is it really a price? Or, is the price paid when our fear prevents us from rising to the opportunity to do our best work and charge higher fees in return? Which choice leads us to greater wealth and deeper satisfaction?

The choice of being willing to add greater value rewards us with more than money. It rewards us with greater satisfaction and increased confidence. These are all higher-ground experiences that encourage us to continue to stretch in our abilities, to add value and in turn attract more money. In this way, being willing to commit can have a tremendous impact on the sustainability of our bottom line and the quality of our lives.

Saying Yes

So often we hear people say, "I wouldn't want to have millions of dollars - what would I do with it all? I would live in fear of the responsibility of so much money." We think, "What?" That's like saying, "I have too much energy and I'm afraid of how I'm going to use it." If you know what you want to do with the energy, how to fully express yourself and get the work important to you done, then this is not a problem. We are afraid because we don't know how to use money intentionally to live the life we desire. If we did, we wouldn't fear the responsibility. We would welcome the ability to augment our highest goals. Being willing is a complicated thing and yet it is easy if the path is right. If the path is right it is easier to simply say "Yes." Accept all of it and be grateful for the stretching and personal growth it will bring. Life has a way of showing you how, as long as you can enthusiastically say "Yes."

"It is not the critic who counts, not the man who points out how the strong man stumbled or where the doer of deeds could have done them better. The credit belongs to the man who is actually in the arena, whose face is marred by dust and sweat and blood; who strives valiantly; who errs and comes short again and again; who knows great enthusiasms, the great devotions; who spends himself in a worthy cause; who at the best, knows in the end the triumph of high achievement, and who, at the worst, if he fails, at least fails while daring greatly so that his place shall never be with those timid souls who know neither victory or defeat. "

— Theodore Roosevelt

Principle #8
You Can't Get There on Empty

- ✓ **Get your needs met ~ become self-ish ~ you can't give what you don't have**
- ✓ **Build reserves in all areas: not having enough reserves can be expensive**

Success Requires a Strong Foundation

- What will you need to have and learn to increase your chances of success?
- You wouldn't think about climbing a mountain without an instructor, and proper equipment.
- The bigger the dream, the stronger the foundation needs to be.

The higher you want to climb, the more strength you'll need.

Whatever your goals for the year, create a system that supports you and guarantees your success.

A multi-step approach:

- A vision or dream that is worthy of you;
- A written plan to guide you;
- Allies and guides who will help you with your plan. Know the difference between supportive people and those who will pull you off your course;
- A coach to support you on the way;
- A chart or graph to mark your progress;
- The equipment or tools you require for success;
- Time to review and renew your determination every day.

An example:

The dream: Create the opportunity of making and investing $100,000.

The Plan contains various strategies:

1) Idea for a new product.
2) Increase income by $10,000 per year.
3) Inheritance money invested...not spent.

Allies: Your best friend who has great ideas for a product that is useful and unique.

Coaching: Business associate who has patented an idea. Accountant and financial planner who can help you set up the money plan for the new business. Coach specializing in entrepreneurs.

Chart: Story board or map with all the ideas, and a tracking system for timelines and pieces of the project.

Equipment and supplies: Sources for the parts of the product. Packaging ideas and experts. Computer spread sheets to track expenses and sales.

Time: One hour per evening to review and refine the plans. Design time for the product. Sales training time, and time to solicit leads for sales.

Tools for Success

Once you know what you will need to achieve a specific goal, you will be able to take the next step and accept the responsibility for creating strong boundaries in your life to enable you to achieve your dream. A boundary is a line you draw around you that protects your Self, your heart and soul. Creating significant boundaries around our needs is an essential skill. However, many find this challenging. Women in particular have been conditioned to put the needs of others first. Overcoming this conditioning can take some effort initially, as you make the paradigm shift from looking after the needs of others to getting your own needs met. You will find that as you do this many of your problems will begin to naturally disappear. You will begin to realize how many personal problems are automatically solved once you establish appropriate boundaries around your needs.

One important way of establishing personal boundaries is to raise your standards, not just for yourself, but for those you work with. For example, if you have a standard that if you are not early, you are late, this is a rule of operating in your own life. Once you define that, you then identify your boundary. Your boundary might be that it is unacceptable to be late. You therefore create extra windows of time so that you are not rushed and pressured. Likewise if someone is late meeting you, then you are able to communicate clearly that you have a standard of timeliness. Their being late is infringing on one of your boundaries. Make it clear that in the future you would greatly appreciate their respect and honor of this. Make timeliness matter when they are meeting you. If it happens again, then you can express yourself more forcefully. It may reach a point that you have to make the decision to end the relationship or forego meetings, if this person continues to dishonor your standard.

A standard is the tone or expectation you set for yourself in a specific area. Raising a standard raises your level of excellence or expectations. An example, you might set a standard that people speak the truth around you, versus saying things they think you want to hear. We get caught up in the superficial social language that our culture has taught us. When someone compliments you or praises you, say, "Thank you, and what I would love is for us to have meaningful conversation. I would love to discuss the things that truly matter to you; will you share them with me?" People will either go deeper and discuss real issues with you, or turn and run in the other direction.

Use the principle of Kaizen to strengthen boundaries a little at a time. This helps others adjust to them. Begin experimenting with the boundaries you set. You'll be surprised to see how raising your boundaries in different areas makes you feel stronger, more self-confident... it's very attractive.

The Climber's Voice:

"When I decided to make sure my need for space and time was met before I made commitments to others, it was a little scary. I was afraid people would think I was selfish and unreliable, but the opposite turned out to be true; I got more respect and people told me they valued my contributions more than ever."

Become Self-ful

"Self-love, my liege, is not so vile a sin as self-neglecting."

— William Shakespeare

Fill yourself up by focusing on caring for your self! Selfishness is the gateway to generosity - you can't give what you don't have.

Are You Being Selfish Enough?

Do you take enough time for yourself?

- We often get so caught up living our busy lives, satisfying other people's needs, volunteering, reacting to everything that comes up, that we don't take the time to focus on ourselves. If you're often too exhausted at the end of the day to spend some quality time focusing on yourself, you are cheating yourself of the energy you require to expand yourself and evolve, and therefore cheating the world of your best self.

- It is easy to fall into the trap, especially when we have young children or an otherwise demanding family life, of thinking that we will be acting selfishly if we take some extra time to be with ourselves. The truth is that the peace and growth you will find as a result of such "selfishness" could be the greatest gift you have to give to your loved ones.

"You cannot give what you don't have."

— Dr. Wayne Dyer

- The risk associated with this is that if you don't take the time and make the effort you may never discover the music in your heart. The world needs volunteers, but the world also needs people who love what they do and do it with unquestionable passion.

- Create space for this work in your life. Find a place where you feel most at peace.

Sarah created space:

"It sounded crazy and felt impossible when my coach suggested that I take one hour per day for myself. Where would I get that hour. I had a full-time job, two kids, a husband, and a full set of commitments to groups and charities. And I

needed sleep. Where would I get an hour for myself. Then with work, and strong coaching, I began to see that I was not taking the time and space to develop myself. I was exhausted because I was doing everything for everyone else.

I joined the 5 o'clock club. I set my alarm early, and dragged myself out of bed. I learned to journal. I even tried meditating, in the beginning falling asleep. I reviewed my goals, outlined my day. And all this in the quiet of the house before anyone else woke up. Then I showered, and began to get the kids up and going. The morning chaos that we used to have felt easier. I was more calm getting to the office. I was also setting goals and plans for me - things I had said I wanted to do, and was feeling frustrated that I hadn't done. I realized I was taking my resentment out on my husband and kids.

My life feels different, and I realize it is all because I am taking time for myself. Without investing in myself, how can I be the best mom, coworker and spouse?"

Imagine you have a cup of water. If you keep subtracting from the water and giving it to others without replenishing it, eventually you will run out of water and will have nothing more to give. There is an alternative that is more sustainable - it requires only a paradigm shift. Instead of depleting your reserve of water to give to others, you continually fill the cup and share the perpetual overflow with all those around you.

The Climber's Voice:

I have found that I'm more inspired and more generous when my needs are met: I then automatically share my inspiration and strength with others. It is when I neglect my own needs that I put my journey at risk and begin to drain others as a result. I have come to realize that the best thing I can do for those around me is to make certain that my own needs are met.

Growing Reserves: Key Steps to Financial Independence

1) Change your thinking to it is possible.
2) Reorient your thinking and spending patterns around the goal of becoming financially independent - not just covering your expenses.
3) Work with a financial planner who understands your values and priorities. Have him or her coach you on all issues that will affect your financial plan and future wealth.
4) Create a high and profitable income stream and/or more than one income stream for greater diversification in income.
5) Build a cash capital reserve.
6) Protect what you have - insuring the assets you have affords you peace of mind.
7) Start living well. Reward yourself by improving the quality of your relationships and life experiences.

Carl was an account manager with a very prominent advertising firm. He had worked hard to get to the top of his field at the early age of 35. He made an impressive six-figure salary and appeared to have the world by the tail, when he was offered an executive position as vice president of international accounts. The job promised a substantial increase in salary, but it would require Carl to be on the road for extended periods of time. Carl was a father of two young boys and the new position would mean that he would not see the boys for weeks at a time. In addition to this, Carl's relationship with his wife was beginning to strain under the demands of his already challenging work and long hours. He knew his relationship with his wife could become irreversibly damaged if he accepted the position, even though initially his wife might be happy about the increase in his pay. The eventual cost of this promotion could be the breakdown of his marriage. Carl decided the benefit of the substantial raise did not outweigh the cost of being away from his family. He took a look at what outcome his decision would likely produce and decided the extra money would cost him too much.

Another way to look at Carl's situation is to see that Carl didn't have the strong foundation he needed to take on the more challenging position. Had Carl strengthened his relationships as he advanced in his career, this next transition might not have been such a difficult one. The feedback Carl received from his wife throughout the years would have been the useful information that he needed to strengthen their relationship. If he had done this he would have created a reserve in his relationship that would have enabled him to stretch himself farther.

When we receive feedback about our actions, it is usually an opportunity to strengthen our foundation to allow us to stretch farther. In a world where continuous change is accelerating, when the demands on us are to continuously stretch ourselves, creating reserves in the core energy areas of our lives (in this case our relationship energy) is essential to strengthening our foundation and securing our future. Think about these core reserves as multidimensional savings accounts of more than enough money, time, space, health, vitality, love, self-confidence and ideas and begin making your deposits daily.

Aspire to Strength

Children know it feels good to be strong. "Show me your muscle," they say. Young children will hike up their sleeves to proudly display their teeny biceps, teeth and fists clenched with the effort. It is thrilling to know your strength and celebrate it. Find ways to do this every day in your own life. Take simple steps!

Steps to Increase Your Financial Strength

- Pay yourself first - set up a savings program.
- Get your needs met - this will increase your intangible assets.
- Be selfish - take care of yourself. This leads to fewer intangible liabilities.
- Invest more - your future depends on it.
- Learn more - increase your compound rate of return from learning.
- Feel like yourself more - you are your greatest asset.
- Become more, need less - increase assets and decrease liabilities continuously.
- Understand abundance - there are more than enough resources in the universe.
- Learn the principles of attraction - by acting like a magnet we can attract any and all of those abundant resources to us. We can literally attract all the people, places and things that we desire into our lives.
- Money energy provides freedom to choose - use money intentionally to create freedom.

Use personal affirmations to keep yourself motivated and focused on increasing your financial strength. Personal affirmations change your self talk. They create positive and powerful statements that become planted in your mind and soul, and eventually create your new reality. They don't actually motivate you - they change your vibration and energy. They are statements that begin with "I am," "I do," "I have."

- I am overflowing with energy and enthusiasm every day.
- I joyfully learn from all my experiences.
- I have all the resources I need for a full and creative life.
- I am attracting wealth.
- I do what it takes to attract wealth and opportunity to me.
- I am a personal magnet that attracts wonderful people, places and things into my life.

There is an important distinction between building reserves and constantly searching for more. In building reserves you are approaching a goal that you have created for yourself out of understanding what is enough. Knowing what is enough gives great freedom - freedom from needless striving, freedom to enjoy your success. The trap of endlessly questing for more is that whatever you achieve will never be enough.

Here are some examples of how to build financial reserves that will support you in creating the life you desire. Notice that most of these include a fixed point that helps you define how much will be enough. Remember there is no freedom in having more, and reserves are primarily about freedom. These are written in the form of affirmations - the present tense: I have, I do, I am.

Money and Freedom:

Build your reserves. Take yourself to the next level:

I always have $100 in my pocket that I never use.

I save/invest 20 percent of what I make each month.

I invest 5 percent of my revenue in my own training.

I have one year's reserve that I don't touch.

I have six months' household and office supplies.

I charge more for my services than I think I am worth.

I am earning a stream of passive income.

I know how much I need to retire/be financially independent and am on that plan.

I have no credit card debt/short term debt.

I make extra principal payments on my mortgage.

I keep at least $5,000 in my checking account.

I tip 15 percent when the service was awful, and tell them this is for training.

I tithe 10 percent to church, charity, friends or those who have made me successful.

I buy the brands I enjoy/like/feel are authentic to me.

Write out your personal list of affirmations in your wealth journal.

Principle #9 Wealth Takes Courage

- ✓ **Courage needs to be nurtured and consciously developed**
- ✓ **Avoiding risk can be risky**
- ✓ **Do something that scares you every day**

Hitting the Wall of Fear

As we journey through life our needs begin to change. We outgrow our current environment and go from being satisfied with our circumstances to being increasingly dissatisfied with where we're at. As we grow, we become inspired by our potential, but we also sense that we need to make changes and this brings on all sorts of anxiety about the unfamiliar. This anxiety is what we call the wall of fear. This is like an imaginary line, which separates where you are now (your comfort zone, the known) and where you want to go (what's possible, yet still unknown). At the wall of fear you will need to make one of two choices.

1) You acknowledge the presence of fear and proceed anyway, going forth with the courage and faith that eventually the new and still unfamiliar will begin to feel comfortable and become the familiar.

or

2) You let the fear stop you from moving forward and you stay immobilized in discomfort and personal stagnation. This is where people get stuck because they are afraid of moving forward in their lives.

You probably know many people who have been held back by the wall of fear. You may identify with this scenario. You don't like where you are and what you're doing, yet you're too comfortable in your discomfort to make any progress toward what you really want. Have you let the illusion of the wall of fear contain you, keeping you from the personal growth that could open up your life?

Be assured that hitting the wall of fear is a natural part of the process of growth and personal evolution - it is simply an automatic reaction to change. It takes courage to step over this illusionary wall and be comfortable with the unknown, but this is required curriculum for success. The good news is that once you do it a few times, you become better at it. You begin to get used to the unfamiliar and you recognize the wall of fear for what it is... an illusion.

> **"When we walk to the edge of all the light we have and take the step into the darkness of the unknown, we must believe that one of two things will happen. There will be something solid for us to stand on, or we will be taught to fly. "**
>
> ***— Patrick Overton, novelist***

Does it take courage at the end of a challenging market cycle to invest money in the stock market? You bet it does. You'll be sweating as you sign your check. But it is precisely at that moment that you have seized the maximum opportunity for return. **Wealth takes courage.**

Aileen

Fear can be both a cause and an effect. A reduction in security or financial reserves can cause worry, and the effect of the worry is that you have less energy to focus on building financial reserves. This is why I disagree with the fear tactics that many people use to sell investment products. The fear can cloud judgment and lead to the wrong kind of action - reaction instead of logical, well-thought-out decisions.

Although it is impossible and, really, undesirable, to eliminate fear completely (because there are times when fear really does protect us from danger) there are concrete actions you can take to reduce fear's power over you.

Reduce Risk

This is not the same as avoiding risk. Reduce risk by:

- Increasing knowledge
- Recognizing truth
- Believing in yourself
- Personal development
- Hard work
- Being organized
- Being prepared
- Building reserves
- Having a plan
- Taking action

All these are behavioral. Financially successful people know that you need to take risks to create wealth. Just as we can reduce risks in our investing, we can also reduce risk in our behavior. This helps us respond to challenges by being prepared and planning ahead, instead of reacting to them in the moment. Like testing the waters before we jump into something new, we can create back-up plans and best-case and worst-case scenarios before making important decisions. The truth is that if we reduce the risk in our behavior, we will not need to take as many risks in our portfolio.

In the journey toward achieving your goals, the greatest risk is that you will give up and get off the path. Failure is only a perception. It may not be seeing the full or larger picture, and the lessons involved along the way. The lessons learned can help us fine tune our approach, and ultimately have greater rewards in the long run.

The process of creating real wealth requires real courage. Exercise your courage muscle by doing something that scares you every day! This is a great affirmation to have in your life and allows you to continually move through your comfort zone.

How Millionaires Overcome Fear

The top 7 actions and thought processes used by millionaires to eliminate and/or reduce fears:

1) Hard work .... 94 percent
2) Believing in myself .... 94 percent
3) Preparation .... 93 percent
4) Focusing on key issues .... 91 percent
5) Being decisive .... 89 percent
6) Planning .... 87 percent
7) Being well organized to deal with big issues .... 83 percent

Source: Table 4-1 *The Millionaire Mind* - Thomas Stanley, Ph.D.

Practice Thinking Abundantly

Abundance means having more than enough. There are more than enough resources in the world. Thinking in those terms allows us to create and attract opportunities, versus blocking things based on our fears of not enough. Scarcity thinking is stock piling food and supplies, based on all the what ifs. This leads us to use more than what we need and takes up energy and time that could be used more effectively.

There are little ways to overcome scarcity thinking in our lives, which will allow us to feel that we have more than enough. For example: we can have more than enough gas by not running the tank down to empty before going to the gas station. Always keep a reserve of gas in the tank. Go to the station when you still have a partial tank of gas. Buy extra supplies. Don't run around the office looking for that last pen and pad of paper. Have extras on hand.

Abundance, like courage, is not denying your fear. It is acknowledging fear and proceeding with faith. The hard times are a fact of life. Learning how to accept them as part of the journey and staying focused on the positive outcome that you desire is an important life skill. We all know people who have every reason to be bitter and resentful for their lot in life. Some, despite their difficulties, have such a positive attitude that you wonder what they know that you don't. These people simply know the difference between what they can control and what they can't. They have the courage to accept their difficulties and the faith that somehow it will all turn out well in the end.

Richard Carlson, Ph.D., and author of *Don't Worry, Make Money* says it is helpful to remind yourself that despite your fears, you are here. Certainly there have been plenty of times when you have been worried in the past, and yet somehow you have managed to survive it all. In this sense all your worries must have been a mirage, a waste of time and energy. The lessons of past fears and worries can help us learn that we are stronger than our fears and more competent than our worries. Next time you begin to worry and let fear interfere with creating what you desire, reflect on past worries and fears. Does what you are feeling seem familiar? Can your doubts be overcome with a little more preparation, a little less risk, a little more faith, a little less attachment to outcome? If you're going to go ahead anyway, if it's something you have to do to get what you want, perhaps you can allow the fear to fall away and proceed.

The Climber's Voice:

There have been times during my journey when I knew I was pushing myself too hard. I knew I needed to stop and catch my breath, but I was so afraid to stop and rest. I feared that if I rested I might lose momentum and not be able to finish, or not finish soon enough. Whenever I eventually took the time to catch my breath I discovered my fears to be unfounded. The rest always rewarded me with better perspective, more energy, more creativity and sometimes a breakthrough that moved me forward and made what came next easier.

Prepare and Plan for Courage

Fear of failure immobilizes us and stops us from daring to live our authentic life. Not having appropriate resources fuels the fears, and blocks us from trying new things.

- Overcome fear with faith and preparation;
- Respond vs. React - Responding to fear is honoring it, allowing it to guide you. Reacting to fear is allowing it to control you
- Autonomy - Automate some of your decisions to enable you to act without constantly confronting fear, like investing monthly.
- Taking on fear is necessary for growth - Fear is a springboard in evolution. Know that you need to take responsibility for managing your fear.

If you choose to let fear shape who you are and what you become, you will be left with the life that your fear restricts you to. Your life experience will be narrow and shallow in proportion to the extent that you let fear govern your life.

What will others think? This is the classic reason many of us live within our social and cultural boundaries. It takes courage to overcome these boundaries.

Courage needs to be nurtured and consciously developed. Recognize this is a muscle that must be exercised if you are to achieve your potential. When you strengthen your courage to live a life that is authentically yours, you will value more and attract more. You will be doing what you need to do and being who you need to be and your confidence and well-being will attract many opportunities. Your energy will be elevated and will begin attracting other energy - including the energy of money.

Developing spiritually can help you build courage and overcome fear by enabling you to see how you are connected to everyone else. This can help you overcome the fear of being alone and lead you to embrace life fully.

"To venture causes anxiety, but not to venture is to lose oneself."

— Senator Orrin G. Hatch

Planning to Reduce Financial Fears

There is fear in not knowing what your financial position is. It is very empowering to know where you are and understand what your strengths and weaknesses are. Knowledge is power - you eliminate fear of the unknown.

- Basic budgeting can help you overcome this fear. It is important for you to know the numbers. Know how much you can spend every week on entertainment, clothes, and all living expenses.

- If you control how much you make (and we all do, really) you need to know how much you need to make every year to cover your expenses.

- Build up your courage by facing the truth. It really will set you free!

In facing the facts perhaps you find you are consistently borrowing from the future to live a certain lifestyle. You could find you literally don't have the income to provide for the way you are living. This requires that you take action, either by reducing your lifestyle or increasing your income. Deciding that you must increase your income may result in your needing to learn certain skills in order to demand more money for the work you do. Perhaps you'll have to commit to your work in a new way to increase your income. If you are not prepared to do this, you may need to reduce your lifestyle to reflect your reality. This can be a difficult pill to swallow, but ultimately very liberating.

Fear of Change

F.E.A.R. is False Expectations Appearing Real. It is our imagination anticipating that something bad will happen. Sometimes this protects us against harm. We try to instill fear in our children to protect them from physical harm. This is why we tell them not to cross the street by themselves, if we know they don't have the skills to do this safely. As adults, most of the fear we experience is in our minds. If we have the skills, then what possible reason do we have to feel fear? Does it make sense for us to feel fear when we can't know for sure that there is something to fear?

Are we just defaulting to fear whenever we don't know what to expect?

How are you holding yourself back? Is there something you want to do but are afraid to take the chance? Change isn't comfortable; it's not supposed to be. However, in order to stretch the limits of our happiness, we must stretch beyond what is comfortable, beyond what we fear. Remember, fear is merely False Expectations Appearing Real. Don't let these imaginary failures keep you from the reality of your happiness.

"Our deepest fear is not that we are inadequate, our deepest fear is that we are powerful beyond measure. It is our light, not our darkness, that most frightens us.

"We ask ourselves, who am I to be brilliant, gorgeous, talented and fabulous? Actually, who are you not to be? You are a child of God. Your playing small does not serve the world.

"There is nothing enlightened about shrinking so that other people won't feel insecure around you. We are all meant to shine, as children do. We were born to make manifest the glory of God that is within us.

"It is not just in some of us; it is in everyone. And as we let our own light shine, we unconsciously give other people permission to do the same. As we are liberated from our own fear, our presence automatically liberates others."

From *A Return To Love: Reflections on the Principles of A Course in Miracles* by Marianne Williamson

"When you want what you want more than you fear what you want, you will receive it."

— Alan Cohen

"The opposite of love is not hate, it is fear."

— Dr. Wayne Dyer

"Life shrinks or expands in proportion to your courage."

— Author Unknown

Exercise:
In your journal, finish this sentence:
"If I had no fear I would..."

Fear of Success

The fear of success is the fear that you will reach your goal but that you will not know what to do beyond that point. Somehow you begin to sabotage your success. It is the fear that you won't be able to sustain what you want to become. The fear of failure, on the other hand, is the fear that you don't have what it takes to succeed.

Challenge these fears. They are only **F.E.A.R.** - False Expectations Appearing Real.

- What is the worst thing that could happen, if you were extremely successful?
- What is the worst thing that could happen, if you were unsuccessful at this attempt?
- How would you handle that?

Look at this list you have created. This is running your life. Will you let it determine your future?

Sometimes we fear achieving our goals. We love the chase so much that we fear our life will become dull if it is too perfect. After all, once you create the life you desire, what will you have to complain about? Once you discover that you have the power to change your life, you will not be able to blame anyone else for the life you have.

Do not be afraid to reach out for help if you need it but never surrender your spirit. Never underestimate your ability to rise above. Have the courage to make yourself more of who you are.

- Take baby steps. Acknowledge your fear, but take small, consistent steps in order to conquer your fear.

- Think about the things you do well. Think about your past successes - let their memory and the confidence they gave you guide you to transcend your present fears.

"If the highest aim of the captain were to preserve his ship, he would keep it in port forever."

Sir Thomas Aquinas

Set sail for your dreams by pulling away from your self-doubt and fear. Life is all about risk. Doing nothing about your dreams may seem safe, but you actually risk everything when you stand still and refuse to take a chance on your happiness. Dreams are meant to be lived and should not be put up on a shelf out of harm's way. When you don't act on your life, you cheat yourself out of not only happiness but also growth. How will you increase your personal power if you do not exercise it? How will you know what you are capable of if you don't even try?

"I will not die an unlived life. I will not live in fear of falling or catching fire. I choose to inhabit my days, to allow my living to open me, to make me less afraid, more accessible, to loosen my heart until it becomes a wing, a torch, a promise. I choose to risk my significance; to live so that which comes to me as seed goes to the next as blossom and that which comes to me as blossom, goes on as fruit."

— Dawna Markova

Principle #10
Life Rewards Action

- ✓ **This is where faith is really put to the test**
- ✓ **Action is a choice - so is not taking action**
- ✓ **You need to plant the seed before you can expect a harvest**
- ✓ **Become a continuous experimenter with life and environment**
- ✓ **Action leads to experience - experience attracts wealth**

Life Rewards Efficient Action

- When we are taking action, our fear is much less.
- Fear begins to disappear as we begin to do. **Just do it!**
- A pendulum doesn't start to swing by itself.
- Many are called - few choose to go.
- Good thoughts alone will not create the life you desire.
- Every decision is a choice, and not acting is also a choice... as is delaying, waiting, stalling, being too busy, avoiding responsibility...etc.

To build wealth, build internal value; then exercise it!

By the time you have arrived at this part of the book you will have a good idea of what your values are, where your passion lies, and a richer sense of your life's purpose. You have been introduced to a number of important concepts in financial planning and life coaching. We hope these concepts have contributed to strengthening your internal framework and have inspired you to begin designing your life around what matters most to you. Now it's time to begin to "put your money where your mouth is." It's time to begin applying your energy in ways that work efficiently with your internal framework.

Resist the trap of thinking you'll act on all of this when... you have more money... more time... more opportunity... Now it's time to focus on acting out what you know.

Take a look at your actions. Are you taking efficient actions toward wealth? When was the last time you used your money consciously to build more internal value? Have you paid dollars for a course recently in an area of interest to you? Or have you been intrigued by a course, but chose not to take it because you didn't think you could afford it, meanwhile spending money on things that are irrelevant to your future. Have you read some of the latest books in your area of expertise, or have you passed them by. Many people feel they don't have enough time to spend reading - all the while spending time doing things they would rather not be doing. Are you relying on what you learned years ago to continue to provide for you in years to come, fearful of how change will impact your career?

When you apply money energy in ways that expand your internal value, you are taking efficient action. This often brings you greater fulfillment and confidence in the future. In this way you are taking action to create more wealth. Using money consciously to fulfill the desires that bring you greater fulfillment and more confidence and joy is the best definition of wealth we know. You may be tempted to distinguish between this type of wealth and material wealth, but our experience tells us that living a fulfilling life is the only way to make wealth sustainable. This is the advanced lesson of life that our experience with money teaches us every day.

"Don't be afraid your life will end; be afraid it will never begin."

— Grace Hansen

The BOLD Approach

"When you cannot make up your mind which of two evenly balanced courses of action you should take — choose the bolder."

— William Joseph Slim

Before we can choose the bold approach in our lives, we must actually come to the point where we see that we have options. This takes creativity, a positive, energetic attitude in life, and often, breaking free from conformity. Some call this "thinking out of the box".

Too often there are expectations of acting the same way that we always have: going to the same functions or family get-togethers, buying gifts in the same places and for the same people, etc. Conforming to the status quo becomes very evident during the holidays and times of celebration within our families. This also happens at work. How often do you see a better way, yet remain silent and go along with the way things have been done in the past? With respect to money, how often do you think, "Why am I paying for all these gadgets and services, when I'm not using them?" Conforming to the status quo often carries high personal costs. How can we expect to close the gap between where we are and where we want to be if we don't use our energy consciously and intentionally toward our highest goals?

Ask yourself how much energy (money, time, vitality etc.) it's taking you to sustain all the things that you are indifferent about. What actions can you take to redirect that energy toward what truly matters to you right now? Understand that in many ways we travel the road to true wealth alone, as individuals, each climbing our own mountain. This is the true meaning of the saying, "It's lonely at the top." True wealth is never achieved by following the herd and depending on others. It is most often attained by following your own path. Lead yourself and do small things with meaning, purpose and direction.

To make changes, we must take meaningful action. As we evolve and become more empowered in our lives, the true tests will come. There will be situations where you no longer feel comfortable accepting the status quo. This is a by-product of greater personal awareness, a result of the higher standards and the stronger boundaries that come with it. Embrace these times as positive affirmations that you are making progress and take the action you know is necessary to stay congruent in your thoughts. Often it feels that it would be easier to just put up with the way things are, not rock the boat. Consider that when we do this we rob ourselves of our power to create the life we desire. If we choose to not take action and in this choice we begin to silence the music within.

Action does not always mean power and aggression - the type of action we see in the movies. It can be simple, quiet, and balanced. It is merely the process of beginning to express our insides on the outside, creating new approaches to how we do things in our lives or speaking up where once we remained silent.

Increasing your financial awareness will bring with it the call for you to take more responsibility for how you are using your money. Embrace this as a sign that you are evolving and are now prepared to play the game of life at a higher level.

We believe:

Intent + Focus = Action

By having the thought, or intention of something, and coupling this with focus and creativity, we see the expression or action happen. So change can be accomplished by changing our thoughts and adding focus and intensity to these thoughts by doing subtle things in our lives. We begin to see the expression of these changes in the form of action.

What simple things would you love to change in your life? What tone or mood would you love to bring to your relationships? How can you begin to create these outcomes that you would love to see? Remember the Principle of Kaizen: if the goal seems too huge, chunk it down until you have identified the first simple step that you can take right now. Begin to do even the smallest things intentionally, aligned with your big picture.

Goethe wrote,"Boldness has genius, power, and magic in it." Be bold in your intent. Add to this some creative focus, some unique approaches, conviction and simple daily changes. This will begin to result in the action: the movement that you would love to see in your life.

Action or movement is all around us. Be bold in your thoughts, your internal dreams. Create the experiences that will be memorable and a true expression of yourself: who you be. Then begin the process of creating the life that you would love.

"Action is the product of the qualities inherent in nature."

— Bhagavad Gita

"Follow your bliss."

— Joseph Campbell

"You can have anything you want if you want it desperately enough. You must want it with an inner exuberance that erupts through the skin and joins the energy that created the world."

— Sheila Graham

Harness the Energy of Inner Exuberance

How can you turn your inner exuberance into the manifestation of your dream? Your inner exuberance is the bubbly surface of a vast well of energy within you. Don't just sit idly by wishing and hoping with all your heart. Get up and take concrete action toward your happiness. Dreams become reality by doing. As your new reality begins to manifest itself in small ways, you will begin to develop real faith: a soul-deep certainty that you will have all you wish for and you will be able to truly commit to doing all that is necessary to make your dreams come true. The real secret of happiness is to believe you can have it. Obey the inner voice that yearns for us to listen and act.

Many people say they have faith, yet are reluctant to take action in their lives. If you had faith that everything would turn out as it should, that all is unfolding for the better, why wouldn't you take the action that you feel strongly could change your life? Once we have taken care of fear by strengthening our foundation, we will need to identify the things that keep us stuck so we can move past them. Often we simply don't trust that we are seeing things clearly and stop ourselves.

The Climber's Voice:

I was certain I could be successful at climbing the mountain,
but I was reluctant to trust that I knew enough to make that assessment,
so I delayed my climb until my faith got stronger.

Isn't that how it works so often for many of us? We're pretty certain we can't possibly know enough to make it, so we don't take action and consequently let opportunities slip by.

Sometimes we think that more learning, more training is required for us to have the confidence to proceed, and sometimes this is true because we do need to be prepared with essential skills to exercise our internal value. However, equally as often, it is one's faith and trust in one's self that needs to be strengthened, not only one's skill. Learning to trust the voice within and be guided by the inner compass we all possess is one of life's most rewarding lessons. You know you are learning this lesson when you begin to see that all you need is already within you. You have only to consider how to use the energy you already have in the right way. And there is nothing to do but to begin. Follow your perception of what is true for you now. Trust and act on the truth you see today. Live fully up to this and you will see more truth tomorrow. Use the energy you have now efficiently and you'll soon know how life rewards action.

"Trust that still, small voice that says,
This might work and I'll try it."

— Diane Mariechild

We need to constantly be reminded that success is an evolutionary concept. We don't begin with perfect knowledge. It is accumulated along the way. The same is true with possibilities. We don't begin our climb knowing that it will lead to many more mountains and heights we never imagined. When we begin our climb we see only the rocks in front of us. We can't predict all the adventures along the way.

We don't see the incredible view from the top that shows us the other mountains on the horizon. We need only begin to take action as a testament of our faith and the universe responds by revealing all... in good time.

Aileen:
"This book was born from a strong sense of purpose that Janice and I shared: to create a guide to help others follow a more holistic approach to creating sustainable wealth and fulfillment in their lives. There were times when I felt stuck and overwhelmed by my vision and its complexity. At different stages of developing Inspired Wealth I questioned my boldness in thinking that I could create something that would contribute to others in a meaningful way. Yet, despite occasional doubt, I felt a strong desire and pull to search for solutions and find clues to facilitate holistic approaches to helping people with money, life and wealth. Had I turned my back on this voice and not taken action, you would not be reading this book. And, I would not have known the true joy of trusting my voice to guide my actions.

"The small actions made the greatest difference. It was the small act of taking my desire seriously that led me to the office of Dr. Janice Hughes, where I came to strengthen my health so I could shoulder this work. It was this small action, which enabled me to receive Janice's coaching and led to a partnership, which in turn strengthened and expanded my vision. It was a decision to become trained to help people through sudden money experiences that was a catalyst in deepening my understanding of the impact of money in our lives. It was the decision to take part in the Nazrudin Project, a think tank of like-minded financial planners, that put me in an environment which nurtured my thoughts and affirmed for me the value in proceeding with this work. It was the small action of writing out my intention that inspired me to develop a framework of thought about using money intentionally and finally led to this book. It was the small action of picking up the phone after a frustrating day and dialing a number I received months before that led to finding John Stevens, the editor, and supporter of *The 12 Principles for Financial Leadership,* who helped us shape this book and get it into your hands. It was the small decision to quiet my mind, not give in to my doubts and instead take action in ways that were congruent with my purpose, that have taught me what I needed to learn in order to help others. It was the continuous action and experimentation in using my energy intentionally in ways that are congruent with my inner values and desires that have empowered me to help others do the same.

Each one of these small actions led me to greater clarity of an ever-expanding vision. I could not have anticipated in advance how it all would come together. I only could trust that I needed to take the next step and climb the rock in front of me."

Don't kid yourself, this book will help you with awareness and clarity, but you still have to take action. Good thoughts alone will not create the life you desire.

Legendary football coach Vince Lombardi put it best when he said, "A champion plays under all conditions." You have to play. That's what you're here for.

Become a Continuous Experimenter

Begin to experiment constantly

We never truly know how the things we do will ultimately impact us. The only way to know for certain is to try. Learn to play the game of continuous experimentation. Stay detached from attaining a particular outcome, instead simply observe what does happen and refine your intuition and subsequent efforts. Plant many seeds and see which of them grow. Don't put all your hopes in one seed. Allow the seeds to develop and grow in their own time, while you consciously observe and nurture them. You may be surprised by the harvest that results and how the collaboration of others increases your bounty.

Experiment in designing your environments

Our environments can support or distract us depending on what we create or allow into them. Experiment with the choices you make about your environment and consciously create environments that support you.

Experimentation leads to experience and experience is a valuable thing to have. You can arrange for experience. You can create an environment that is conducive to the experiences. You can in this way attract more experiences. This is what planning is all about. It is about shaping the experiences that will in turn shape you. Experience helps us speak with authority. Experience helps us lead others, as everyone looks for experienced guides along their journey. Always look for ways in which you can act to elevate your experience of life to one of using your energy intentionally to attain your highest goals.

Principle #11 The Present is Perfect

- ✓ **The present is an efficient feedback mechanism - it's perfect to learn and grow from**
- ✓ **The sooner you learn the greater is your compound rate of return from learning**
- ✓ **The present contains the full potential of our future**

"Our history is not our destiny."

— Alan Cohen

What happens when things don't go our way?
If you don't achieve your goals, does the plan break down?

Your life is full of defining moments. From joy to sorrow, from pleasure to regret, life can be beautiful one day and filled with heavy burdens the next. Don't let this take you off your path. Cherish the joys in your life and, when faced with difficult times, make up your mind that you will not let circumstance determine your happiness, your success, or lack thereof. Make up your mind that you will define the moments in your life. Be courageous and be willing to trust that your inner strength will blossom as you meet your challenges with an unwavering heart.

The Climber's Voice:

"There were times when I was truly exhausted, so drained from the challenges of each step that I questioned my ability to finish the climb. The top seemed so far away and I had already given all that I thought I could. At these times I thought, 'Where will I find the strength to continue? How much longer can I keep going? Who did I think I was to embark on such a difficult journey anyway?"

"Funny thing... whenever I asked such a question the answer appeared. It came to me in many forms: sometimes in the form of an unexpected kindness from a fellow climber; other times it was something I read along the way - I would open to exactly the page I needed to read at that precise moment. However, the most powerful inspiration came when I chose to listen to the small voice from within that encouraged me to keep going, assuring me that if I kept putting one foot in front of the other I would eventually find my way. I began to trust the saying, 'When the student is ready, the master will appear,' and I began to know that 'Seek and you shall find' was not an empty promise. I knew that this voice would carry me to the top of the mountain. My role was to listen when it spoke and continue putting one foot in front of the other."

Learn from each step. Be consistently open to the lessons of each day, hour and minute. Living in the present, accepting the past, honoring the future. See the opportunity that is built into the present of each day.

The past is behind you, the future unknown; the only true gift is the present.

List your five greatest challenges in your journal.

1)______________________________

2)______________________________

3)______________________________

4)______________________________

5)______________________________

Now imagine that you have already reached your goals and are standing victoriously on top of the mountain. Look back along the path you travelled to this place. What did each of these challenges teach you along the way? How did they serve you on your journey? What did you need to learn to overcome and outgrow them? What did you gain from each of these perceived setbacks or challenges? We can easily get stuck in the muck - focusing on our perception of the challenge as a problem, a defect or a barrier. By embracing a bigger vision of the future, as if you were already there, you can be objective and see the new skills and pieces that you are learning from these precious challenges.

A wonderful Chiropractor and healer was feeling stuck. She was practicing success principles, saying affirmations every day, setting her practice up to add true value and healing to her patients - and yet she continued to struggle. Her business was barely surviving. She wanted to be thriving! In the early stages of the struggle she blamed many things outside of herself - the location, the economy, her advertising, her staff. One day she realized this was about herself. She began working with a coach to identify the things that were blocking her success. Bit by bit she was making changes, yet her practice was still barely surviving. One day she woke up knowing that she didn't love the place she was practicing in. It was close to her family, her lifelong friends. Yet she realized that she had talked for years of moving to the mountains, living in a place that fueled her soul. This was something she had been putting off until she made it. Her language about this was, "When I am successful, with a great practice, I will sell it and move to the mountains." On that day she suddenly realized it was time to act as if she were successful. Why not move to where she truly wanted to be? Within two months she had sold her practice to a newly graduated Chiropractor, moved to the mountains, started a practice 3 days a week, and she was able to ski in the winter and hike in the other seasons. Looking back on the days of exhaustion and frustration, she says, "Instead of asking myself the powerful questions, I kept blaming everything else for the situation I was in. Only when I thought of the big picture of what I would love, and began to see that the lessons of being stuck were about myself, and not other people and circumstances, did I realize that I could make changes. There are still many days that bring challenges and obstacles - the difference is that now I embrace them. I realize that the faster I learn my lessons, the more quickly I get to continue to live and love each day!"

Learn to detach from the problem and see the wisdom and how the learning has become part of your journey.

Reset Your Compass

We are on a 40-mile sail with an automated GPS system guiding our course. We must take periodic readings on the GPS and slightly change our course accordingly. The wind, the waves, and the technical limitations of the boat will all gradually take us slightly off the course we have set. If we do not periodically make appropriate adjustments, we will be well off the target we had originally set, and maybe in serious trouble, by the end of the voyage.

"The method of the enterprising is to plan with audacity, and execute with vigor; to sketch out a map of possibilities; and then to treat them as probabilities."

— Christian Nevell Bovee

Your life experience begins within and always takes place in the present. We don't experience things in the past or in the future. The present is really the only time we have. What you choose to think and believe about people and events determines the very nature of your experience: these are the choices that shape your future. In the same vein, how you respond to life determines your happiness or unhappiness. You can either choose to wait for good things to happen to you or you can be audacious and shape your future by navigating the opportunities of the present, making wonderful things happen for you instead.

Maintaining a positive attitude in today's world takes focus and dedication. It's easy to get caught up in the negative energy if you are not vigilant. The newspapers and television are full of negative headlines and images. We are bombarded by negative information because negative headlines sell. It's human nature to pay more attention to the things we fear: this is a survival mechanism that kicks in to protect us from danger. However, too much of this is equally dangerous. Negative messages can pull us off our intended paths. You will need to choose your environment carefully and continually choose to focus on the gifts of the present. Choose to believe in the best possible outcome for yourself and commit to making it a reality now.

"What lies behind us and what lies before us are tiny matters compared to what lies within us."

— Ralph Waldo Emerson

What lies within each of us is a capacity for personal greatness. But it is neither our past disappointments nor our fear of the future that keeps us stuck in place, rather it is our inability to act now. More often than not we lack not just courage but a fundamental belief in ourselves that would enable us to act in the moment. It is much easier to nurse old hurts and anticipate future failures than it is to do something about our happiness right now. But we are fortunate: within each of us is the strength to face this truth about ourselves and to get up and do something about creating our happiness every day, beginning in this moment.

Why not begin to think about the things that you would love to bring into your life in the next year? There is no better way to begin this process than to look at the year you have just created.

Has this year been everything you had planned or hoped it would be? Look carefully at all areas of your life. Have you focused on your whole life, or have you been caught up and only focused on the crisis areas? The river of life flows so quickly these days it is easy to get caught up in only a few pieces of our lives. Only in review do we stop and realize there were many things we have neglected.

Months and weeks fly quickly by. If we do not create a strategic plan and focus for ourselves, we reach the end of another year wondering why we have not put time and energy into the things we say are important to us.

Applying This to Money.

The present is perfect because it is full of choice. Financial leadership lies in our ability to choose intentionally with the money energy we have today.

It is quite astonishing the amount of money that flows through our hands in our lifetime. It boggles the mind that many of us make millions of dollars over the course of our working years. However, as we all know, the money flows through quickly, often without our directing it to the things that matter most to us. Become aware of the danger of missing your opportunity to create wealth in your life because you continuously look to do it tomorrow. What would it take to direct some of this energy toward your highest goals and deepest values right now? What choices would you need to make right now?

What is important to you? Which areas of your life have you been neglecting, or finding no time for over the last few months or years? How would you like this to be different in this coming year? Often work fills so much of our lives. If the company is moving in a certain direction, then so are we. Is this really where you would like to be moving?

Take this time to put the focus on your most critical business - *your life!*

Before any thought of change, we must review and accept where we have been. Pull out those goals you originally wrote for yourself last year - or even 10 years ago. Please don't beat yourself up over this, simply review what you said was going to be important to you. We have all changed over the years. Consider that your capacity to attain these goals may have also evolved and that perhaps it's now time to renew your commitment to your vision. Simply use this list to highlight the things you have already accomplished and decide if there are any goals you would like to refocus your energies toward. Use this as a stepping-stone to begin to think through what you would like to create for the upcoming year.

Giving >>>>>>Receiving>>>>>>Gratitude
Gratitude Enables You to Manifest Your Goals

Your gratitude attracts that which you are grateful for. Be grateful for all you will receive - this is a declaration of belief that builds a calm knowing that what you want for yourself will materialize - it's just a matter of time and focus. Trust that what you want also wants you. This brings confidence that is also attractive.

Be grateful for everything that materializes for you and everyone who comes into your life because everything in your life helps you discover an aspect of yourself. This is the holistic approach. All of life serves to make you better. Seeing life this way is very powerful - it conquers fear.

". . .the more you become a connoisseur of gratitude, the less you are a victim of resentment, depression and despair."

— Sam Keen

The trick is to learn to want everything that you already have, to love the present moment. Doing this places you in a state of calmness and in a position most suited for finding the gifts contained in the present so you can rapidly grow in the direction you wish to move. Faith is the gift that gratitude brings.

Janice:
"I had known, and taught other people for years, the power of thankfulness and gratefulness. Yet was I truly taking the time in my own life to be thankful for everything? With my crazy schedule I would often be exhausted at the end of the day. I would come up with a general thought of being thankful and leave it at that.

"One night I stopped in my tracks on our stairs as I heard my husband tucking in our five-year-old. They were discussing the day, and a mean kid who had said something nasty to my son. My husband, in his calm and easy way, asked my son what he was thankful for that day. There was quiet in the room. He again asked my son what great things had happened to him. Slowly my son began to talk about getting picked to be first in line for recess, a nice thing one of his friends said, and a couple of other small pieces from his day. My husband asked him if he would like to play a game each night, called 'night time thankfuls.' I sat and cried as I realized how powerful this quiet moment had been - my husband had balanced my son's day. He had taken a sad, negative energy, and turned this into an exercise for my son to balance each day, and go into a restful sleep focusing on all the wonderful things in his life. This is an exercise that we continued consistently with our son, and later with his brothers. My all-time favorite was his being thankful for 'bluejay ice cream' - his favorite flavor at the time. To this day, as I wish on a star, or wish on a milkweed feather, I wish for more bluejay ice cream in my life. By being thankful for all the little things, including flavors of ice cream, it has brought riches to my life."

How do you handle NOT accomplishing a goal?

This is the point in the hero's journey where he must wrestle with demons - the point of greatest peril and the point of greatest opportunity. We have heard it said, "Where you stumble, there your treasure is." So what if this is your story. You have set goals, reached for the stars, and apparently come up empty! Now what? Do you get turned off and tell yourself there is no hope, no point in goal setting?

Why not take a closer look at what happened? Did you set goals that were not congruent with your values? Did you self-sabotage out of a fear of what would happen if you actually got what you want? Did you lack the faith to keep on going in the face of obstacles? There could be one major reason behind your not accomplishing your goal - or there may be many.

This does not mean that goal setting does not work. It may simply mean that it is time to break down barriers within yourself. It may also mean that you have to chunk down your goal into manageable bits and pieces. A goal may be so large that it will take years to come to fruition. Why not break it down into smaller pieces that can happen in time frames to give you the feedback that this goal setting approach can actually work.

The Climber's Voice:

Seeing life as a journey can be so helpful. I find that every year around my birthday I am very reflective about what I have learned in the preceding year and how far I have come toward my goal. My vision is large enough to last me a lifetime, and the learning required to reach my goal may also take my lifetime! I've chunked down my goals to the lessons that help me develop in attaining various stages of my vision. Each lesson is a triumph and I know it takes me closer to where I want to go.

Remember how important it is to chunk down goals. It is important to take any goal, and break it down into such manageable pieces that you can take some simple action now and today. We can write the goal, which is Intention, yet without bringing instant attention in some way to it, we are not in action. Without action we haven't brought the goal to life. Intention is on the 'be' level, the concept and vision level. Without some action in the present, we will not be moving toward the goal. We must place attention on the details that will enable us to move in the direction of the goal. Even if it is a far-off goal, simple and consistent action steps will keep it alive for us every day.

"Life does not happen to us, it happens from us."

— Mike Wickett

Not accomplishing a goal may also reflect the fact that something else has happened in your life that means your goal is no longer appropriate. As you strive in one direction, there may be things occurring to pull you off path, or in another slightly different direction. Take a closer look. There may be interesting lessons, and even benefits in the change in direction. This is where we can begin to sense that there is a larger design and bigger picture to this universe. It may be that our setting our goal, and moving into action, has attracted other more appropriate things into our life. This is something to celebrate, something to be grateful for. This is why it is imperative that we continue to review our goals. Rewrite your goals based on things that most matter in your life, things that are authentic to you.

Heroic Change of Plan

Earnest Shackleton is remembered as one of the great heroic leaders of all time. When his original goal of crossing Antarctica on foot became unattainable because his ship was trapped and crushed in the ice, he immediately formulated an even more daring vision. He would bring every member of his expedition home alive. On the face of it, it was a hopeless task, and in fact involved several seemingly impossible feats of seamanship, mountaineering and sheer endurance under appalling conditions. But at the end of the long struggle, all his men were safely brought home.

Time Value of Money

The sooner you strengthen your money/life skills the farther you will evolve. The expanding and strengthening and building of reserves you do today will have the greatest impact on your future. This is the law of compound rate of return. We encourage young couples to make sacrifices in lifestyle early in their marriages, to build their reserves and skills. Doing this later in life just doesn't have the same effect. Many opportunities will pass them by because they don't have the resources to take advantage of them. They have traded these opportunities for the privilege of having it all immediately – nice furniture, a great car. Few people realize just how high the opportunity costs can be when we **have** before we **become**. This is all part of the trap of creating a lifestyle versus a life.

Opportunity Costs

Talk about opportunity lost! If you put $5,000 into a toy like a high definition big screen television instead of investing this money in the International Equity Index earning a 10 percent rate of return, you will have forfeited the opportunity to have $20,886 in 15 years, $33,637 in 20 years or $87,247 in 30 years - that's a pretty expensive television! Think of all the real life experiences this money could have facilitated! Was it worth the cost to enjoy that $5,000 toy in the present moment, or would it have been better to wait and have the experiences the money would have bought once it had a chance to grow? You can use this with your Inspired Balance Sheet to come to your own conclusion.

Consider that you will need more future money to have the same value as today - thanks to inflation. For this very reason we need to evolve and add more value just to stand still!

The Time Value of Life Skills

It is easy to illustrate the time value of money. It is perhaps not so obvious that the same applies to life skills. Develop the capacity to treat the present as a valuable feedback device. Hear the story your life is telling you and the lessons you are learning. Create the emotional reserves of a dynamic relationship. Greet each experience as an opportunity. The sooner you can begin to compound your life skills the more positive effects you see on your journey to inspired wealth.

Principle #12
There Are No Limits

- ✓ **Our ability to create makes us "un-limited"**
- ✓ **Avoid judging what's possible**
- ✓ **Continue to grow and enrich your life**

Become "Un-limited"

After wrestling with his demons and achieving his ambition, the hero returns with his treasure, and the community rejoices. He has come back safely, he has brought valuable gifts. They are reassured of the rewards of the journey, their fear is quieted and their faith strengthened. The hero has led the way.

But the call to adventure is strong. The real gift the hero has brought back is knowledge - self knowledge and knowledge of the deep secrets of the world. He has learned that there are no limits - no limits for the bold who will heed again the call to adventure and set out to discover what the wide world has to give them.

The stories he tells around the fire at night rekindle his desire to set out on the adventurous path. They also kindle that flame for the first time in the hearts of the young. If the community is fortunate, at least one of them will set out for unknown lands along uncharted paths and bring back more treasure, more wisdom, and a spark to light that fire in others. There is no end to the adventure of self-discovery.

We Believe:

- We impose limits on ourselves, so we can let go of them too.

The ability we have to create helps us to continuously re-create ourselves to become what we want. In this sense we are truly unlimited. All we have to do is declare our intention powerfully and follow through with commitment. We will make our visions happen. It's what we're designed to do.

Consider this: In this fast-paced, digital, global world, our ability to re-create ourselves is becoming a significant asset and a sought-after leadership trait. Perhaps we should be grateful that the days of working at one career throughout the course of our lives are gone. There are great gains to be made in creativity and innovation when you are able to apply what you learn from one career or discipline to another. This is synthesis. It expands one's perspective just as a wide-angle lens expands a camera, helping us see a broader picture and simultaneously see the opportunities for greater understanding. Synthesis is a valuable and learnable skill. All one has to do is become conscious of its potential and begin applying it at every opportunity.

"The world is moving so fast now-a-days that the man who says it can't be done is generally interrupted by someone doing it."

— Elbert Hubbard

Committing to continued growth on your personal path can help you raise the lid on your conditioning. Don't get stuck! If you put grasshoppers in a jar with a lid, the grasshoppers will quickly become conditioned to only jump so high in the jar as to not bump their heads on the lid. You would think that after your remove the lid, they would recognize the opportunity to jump out of the jar. However, apparently they don't. Their conditioning keeps them jumping at the same height for some time despite the fact that they are free to jump right out of the jar. In the same way our own conditioning often keeps us stuck. It's up to us to become aware of what limits us and make the continuous effort to challenge it.

Two frogs fall into a pit along the path. Their companions yell down to them: "Give up, you can't get out!" They begin to jump to try to get out. It is too deep. At first they jump and jump, trying to jump higher with each jump. Finally they fall down exhausted. The frogs above continue calling down for them to give up, they can't make it, etc. One of the frogs gets up, and resumes his jumping. The frogs above call louder and louder, telling him to give up. The frog in the pit only increases his jump height a bit each time, and all seems hopeless, until suddenly there is a miracle jump - and out hops the frog. The others are astounded, crowding around and screaming with delight. When things finally quiet down, they ask how he did it, where did the incredible jump come from. The frog shares with everyone that he is almost totally deaf, and he assumed the calls and screams from the others were cheers and support. Even when he thought he had nothing else to give, and saw them cheering, he knew he had to dig deep within himself. He has no idea where the miraculous jump came from, the one that allowed him to fly out of the pit. It seemed his body dug into stores of strength he never knew he had to help him fly out of the pit!

Avoid Judging What's Possible

Remember that there was a time when we didn't think the fax machine or the internet or many other new developments were possible or practical. People at the turn of the century thought electricity was a fad, that everything that could ever be invented already was. We will always be wrong when we underestimate man's ability to create and adapt.

Think about how often you have underestimated your own ability. Most of us periodically have the experience of being surprised by our own achievements. We embark on a goal and soon after realize it is the bridge to other even more exciting opportunities. How often do we say things like, "Thank goodness I did that because if I hadn't, it wouldn't have led me to do this." Commonly, the second possibility was not visible before embarking on the first goal. This is what we call a "Bridge To Re-Vision". It's the new vision that continues to generate itself after we take action toward our goals. The Bridge To Re-Vision is a metaphor for the ever-expanding possibilities of life, always there if you are willing to see.

Retirement Without Limits

New advances in medicine mean that we will be retired longer. Retirement has to be redefined by who we are and the growth we want to achieve in this rich part of our lives. Scientists and many seniors are pushing the limits of our longevity.

This brings new possibilities and new challenges for all of us. It is time we reconsider the idea of retirement in our society and our own needs as we approach this transition, not just economically, but also the need to continue to learn the skills of re-creating ourselves in a changing world. Longer life will demand participation where the custom in retirement historically has been withdrawal. This means more activity for an expanded number of years and a paradigm shift from retiring from something to transitioning to something new - not an end, but rather another beginning. This truly is a time of re-creation.

One of the fringe benefits of our progressive world is that an increasing number of people are compelled to dream bigger. A longer lifespan can enable us to choose to have bigger goals and visions and become more experienced at achieving them. The analogy of the climber's journey applies as much to our retirement years as it does to our working years. As a matter of fact, it is likely a recipe for vitality. More and more evidence suggests that keeping one's dreams alive and one's vision big is an important element of vitality and an effective preventative measure against dis-ease and depression. This affirms the life-giving qualities of continuous "Re-vision" as we adapt to the changing circumstances of our lives.

Financially the changing reality of retirement presents many serious challenges. Greater longevity brings more demands on personal finances at the same time responsibilities for personal pensions and retirement plans are being shifted down from the institutional to the individual level. The need has never been greater for personal financial leadership in our quest to ensure we will be able to remain financially independent throughout our lives and not restricted by lack of money or lack of health. Indeed our health may largely depend on our wealth and vice versa.

The Wealth of Health.

In your Inspired Wealth Journal:

- Take stock of your physical health and wellness.
- What changes can you make today to focus on bringing more health and vitality into your life?
- What is/was the health of your parents? Are you on the same path or road that they were?
- What age do you envision yourself living to, and in what physical condition will you be?
- List 10 daily things you could do for yourself to begin a path that will enable you to have the health you desire, to utilize the wealth you are creating.

Will you be healthy, in great physical condition, to utilize the wealth that you are focused on creating?

Remember:

- Take action congruent with your vision.
- You can have wealth and be successful with money.
- Stay aligned and you'll stay on your path - this is tough sometimes, there will be difficult choices to make, but once you choose, it will be easier than not having chosen.
- Be prepared that others may not understand, and this will challenge what you know to be true.
- What you focus on expands - stay focused on your vision.
- Serendipity happens when you are on the path - the Creator designed us to succeed.

" I have made myself what I am"

— Tecumseh

Growth Is Essential To Life

The purpose of all life is growth, just like the purpose of life for a tree or a plant is to grow. They grow when there is light and when their specific needs are met. We have some specific physical needs, such as food (nutrition), water and oxygen. There are many other examples of more extensive needs in our lives. We too grow when we get our specific physical, mental and spiritual needs met and when we seek out light, which is clarity, purpose, love and service.

"When you were born, you cried and the world rejoiced. Live your life so that when you die, the world cries and you rejoice."

— Cherokee Saying

The Process as a Circle

If we expand our vision about money and think about wealth creation and our financial well being as financial leadership, we can create a continually evolving and proactive process for ourselves. Even with career changes, life changes, or other things that impact our initial financial plan along the way, we can reinvent ourselves and determine to lead ourselves to attain our highest goals.

Take a look at the diagram on the previous page: Financial planning is a never-ending cycle. It is important to realize that the review and revision step takes us right back to the first step of gathering and assessing data. You can enter at any point, and you can continue on throughout your life as you learn and grow. Embrace financial planning as a process of self-discovery and evolution. This is an inner game that gets played out in the nitty gritty of decision-making, when we ask ourselves questions like: Should I save it or spend it? How much will I need? How much should I give? Should I take the risk? All of these questions are about our identity. They are deeply personal, and as intimate as money can be.

Here is a Flow Chart For Sustainable Wealth Creation

Identify Values

▼

Create Vision

▼

Identify Goals

▼

Identify Problems

▼

Develop Plans

▼

Select Strategies

▼

Align Energy (Money, Enthusiasm, Effort, Faith)

▼

Monitor Results and

▼

Revise or Fine-Tune

Financial planning is about money and life. It is about faith and hope and authentic vision. It's about growing and *evolving* throughout our lives.

Review and Revision

How often do you review your plan? Your basic plan can be something that you understand easily and can identify with at all times. This is the only way you will know whether your day-to-day decisions are congruent with your intentions. Simplify the financial planning process. Make this practical and easy.

You can begin to create a basic outline right now. All you need to do is consider what you need to do to strengthen your personal and financial foundation right now. Then think of your vision for the future. What will need to happen for you to close the gap between where you are now and where you want to be according to that vision? Then consider the things you will face along the way and begin thinking about how you can eliminate these threats by preparing for their impact.

Of course, we strongly recommend you see a financial planner to help you discover the impact of your assumptions: the amounts of money you will need to save and invest along the way to achieve your goals, as well as the size and nature of the potential pitfalls you may encounter, and how to plan to prevent them from undermining your efforts.

Unfortunately, when it comes to financial planning, what you don't know may hurt you and what you know a little about may hurt you even more. So be certain to get qualified professional advice when creating your plan. However, doing a simple trial on your own can be a valuable exercise. It will get you thinking about some of the important issues that will likely come up in the planning process. This will make you better prepared to get the most from your financial planning engagement.

An even more powerful approach is to have a financial coach. Coaching is a process that literally helps you create the action steps and pieces that will take you from where you are to where you would love to be. Currently in the financial planning arena there are some coaches who have the background of a financial planner, and have linked financial planning with coaching as we have in this book. They have re-created the traditional approach and offer a more holistic approach to financial success. These individuals will ask you powerful questions, help you create steps and pieces along the path, to attain the vision you have for your future and finances.

Transition: A Constant Companion

Sometimes significant changes to your plan may be required and they usually occur at times of transition in our lives. This may be when we feel we are no longer growing in our present situation. We might know it's time to take the next step yet it still brings up fears and challenges. Life may show us the next step as a result of a significant event that occurs. Whatever actually creates the time of transition in your live, this is an important time to review and revise a financial plan. Your plan enables you to make responsible decisions based on the realities of the present. Revising the plan, or creating a new one if there is no financial plan in place, is a valuable process particularly during times of transition. It can clarify your needs and make the solutions obvious. This simplifies the decision-making process and creates greater confidence that you are making sound decisions about your future.

Transition is a reoccurring theme for those who live unlimited lives. Some transitions are harder then others. The key to remember is that all transitions are initially uncomfortable. They simply bring us out of our comfort zone. It is through the discomfort that we learn and grow. Those who live unlimited lives, and move in the directions of their dreams, know that discomfort is imperative on the journey. By learning through these stages they grow as people, and move toward their potential.

The journey is like peeling the layers of an onion - the onion is the most potent immediately after you peel a layer off. After some time however the odor is less pungent and the next layer can be peeled. This continued movement through the levels, through the layers or skins of the onion, is what enables us to uncover our true authentic self.

The Climbers Voice:

"As I stretched to reach the top of the mountain I saw that there are many more mountains before me, always another just beyond the horizon. Each one is full of life lessons and adventure, just waiting to call out to me at the precise moment I am ready to listen to the call. At that moment I realized I hadn't just climbed a mountain, I had become a climber of mountains. I was someone who was prepared and willing to take action in faith exploring the full potential of my life. As difficult as the climbing was, I never wanted to stop climbing my mountains. I knew that if I stopped the very part of me that creates the value I add to others would begin to die. "

Learn your lessons fully, then make the changes that are revealed through the lessons. This is a process that is ongoing and a fundamental element of leadership: honor that this is the way to a fulfilling life. Give yourself the space to learn the lessons. Let there be room for the mistakes, don't let them make you stuck. Release yourself from your conditioning and go boldly into your unlimited potential. Share your discoveries and your adventure with others; it is a great gift that has unlimited potential when it is shared. Please know that people are hungry to hear your story. We all are depending on the inspired wealth you can create as a result of your embarking on your journey and fulfilling your quest.

In the heroic myths, the hero is transformed in a struggle that demands more than seems possible. This forces the hero to draw on resources never before used and to deploy existing resources in innovative ways. The victory transforms the hero, who can now return to the everyday world equipped with new skills, attitudes, values and resources.

In our individual lives, the call comes many times. If we are wise and adventurous, we listen, and embark once more on the most rewarding adventure imaginable - the adventure of self-discovery, self-actualization...the quest for inspired wealth.

We encourage you to witness the benefits of financial leadership. Begin to use money intentionally, with meaning, purpose and direction to create the fulfilling life you desire!

"Here is a test to find whether your mission on earth is finished: if you're alive, it isn't.

- Richard Bach

Our wish for you -
May you listen for the whispers in the wind!

Looking Back

We live in the most affluent society in human history, yet we lack the wisdom to use money intentionally to achieve our highest goals.

This book began with this realization. In closing, we believe it is important to come back and address this dilemma again. One of the messages we would like you to take away with this book is the understanding that making money and creating wealth is not enough. It will not save us and lead us to the fulfilling lives we desire. We have to align wealth with our intuition and our true being.

We are often so busy, so worried about building outer value - to have, to retire - that we are forgetting to build inner value. Ignoring the need to build this intrinsic value within ourselves makes outer value (wealth) very difficult to sustain. In the same way, it is difficult for a stock to sustain a high price if its intrinsic value is low - it sometimes works for a while, but eventually the truth comes out.

We all need to tell our story and understand our story to find meaning. Inspired wealth means being able to use both your inner value and outer resources to live your story.

"Money must become a tool in the only enterprise worth undertaking for any modern man or woman seriously wishing to find the meaning of their lives. We must use money in order to study ourselves as we are and as we can become."

— Jacob Needleman

Inspired Wealth

Personal Financial Leadership
For Sustainable Wealth Creation

Growth Resilience Stewardship Vision Authenticity Freedom

"Leadership is a concept we often resist. It seems immodest, even self-aggrandizing, to think of ourselves as leaders. But if it is true that we are made of community, then leadership is everyone's vocation, and it can be an evasion to insist that it is not. When we live in the close-knit ecosystem called community, everyone follows and everyone leads."

— Parker Palmer, Let Your Life Speak

Financial Leadership is a skill that begins with our willingness to gain the competency and build the strength to guide ourselves and accept guidance in our life's journey. Since money touches every aspect of our lives, the concept of individual financial leadership is important to the overall success and well-being of each of us.

Although we hear the term "born leader," more often than not, leadership skills are developed rather than inherited. Leadership exists on a continuum from managing self to managing others to managing an organization. Natural leadership does not mean that you either have it or you don't. It does mean that you are willing to assess your style and behavior, and that you are willing to learn and grow. Leadership is a set of skills and values. The skills can be learned. And through identifying our values, using these new leadership skills and linking them with our vision, magic happens.

12 Principles for Financial Leadership

1) Money = Energy
2) The Truth Will Set You Free
3) Honor Who You Are
4) You Are a Creator
5) Expand Who You Be, Not Only What You Have
6) Let Go & Eliminate
7) Be Willing to Climb Your Mountain
8) You Can't Get There on Empty
9) Wealth Takes Courage
10) Life Rewards Action
11) The Present is Perfect
12) There Are No Limits

We see the *12 Principles for Financial Leadership* as an operating system for personal financial leadership that can guide you to use money intentionally. It is a framework where emotional intelligence meets money and the result is a new **financial intelligence** that penetrates to the heart of the money issues in our lives.

We have used this as a powerful tool in teaching people important money skills. We have also found it particularly useful in working with families where money issues present challenges in communication.

Aileen

Someone asked me recently if it was difficult as a financial planner talking to people about such personal things. I honestly replied, "I have yet to find someone who, if I have the courage to take them there, is not interested in learning more about themselves and using their energy in an intentional way, congruent with who they truly are to create the life they desire." Interesting how we all think that others are different than ourselves, when the truth is that we are all searching for more meaning, purpose and joy in our lives.

What We Believe

- We believe that people increasingly want to find greater meaning in their lives and attain their highest goals. They want to begin using money intentionally to create the lives they desire.

- We believe that it is time to recognize the link between creating wealth and increasing personal development.

- We believe that financial peace is the ultimate status symbol.

- We believe that the financial planning process is inherently a process of self-discovery and personal evolution.

- We believe that wealth creation requires that we focus on behavior and that financial planners will increasingly begin to integrate coaching skills into their practices to satisfy their clients' needs for creating sustainable wealth.

- We believe that financial planning is an essential life skill and that expanding public awareness about using money intentionally is a valuable endeavor.

- We believe that all individuals in society can evolve and create value through the understanding of their values and how they connect to their resources. We see this as an inspiring formula for sustainable wealth creation and the answer to many challenging problems in today's society.

- We believe that financial leadership is an essential survival skill for the 21st century.

Our ability to use money intentionally is the key to the evolution of the human spirit and the inner wisdom we all possess that yearns to be developed for the purpose of guiding us.

Who are the Heroes?

They are those who choose to climb their mountains: the entrepreneur who believes in his vision and goes for it; the executive who encourages new ways to solve old problems; the parent who teaches by being an example of how to live a fulfilling life; the teacher who inspires self-discovery and personal evolution; the artist who manifests his expression; the professional who endeavors to see beyond the limits of his own discipline and applies holistic approaches to help individuals reach balance and integrity in all areas of their lives.

The Archetypical Hero's Journey with Money

Joseph Campbell, in *The Power of Myth*, spoke about the significance of the hero's journey. He described the hero's journey, not as an outwardly courageous act but as a life in self-discovery. Ironically, to Campbell the end of the hero's journey is not the aggrandizement of the hero. It is not to identify one's self with the powers experienced. "The ultimate aim of the quest must be neither release nor ecstasy for oneself, but the wisdom and the power to serve others;" to add value. Campbell distinguishes between the celebrity and the hero, by pointing out that one lives only for self while the other acts to redeem society.

In the same way your quest toward inspired wealth will not mean that you will be immediately rewarded with material wealth. However, our experience and the experience of many throughout human history tell us that you will gain valuable wisdom and new power to serve others. Modern society is needing you to take this journey. Please say "Yes," it's worth it!

Remember:
Money = Energy, it is what connects us through the value we add, not what separates us. You may find that your ability to share your new found wisdom will eventually attract more money and reward you in multiple ways: physically, emotionally and spiritually.

Use Money Intentionally

- Use money to expand who you are.
- Use money in ways that support your goals.
- Use money in ways that leverage results.
- Use money to build a strong and solid foundation.

Use money intentionally to say "yes" to the call!

Ironically, at the time we were completing this book we experienced the biggest blackout in North American history. We are finally beginning to understand that we are stewards of the world's resources. The truth is that they are not all renewable. This has spurred much discussion lately about how we are using energy. It's time we begin to understand that we are also stewards of our time, treasure and talent. The world needs us to pay greater attention to how we use all our energy, including money. We cannot ignore the stewardship of wealth any longer. It is time to evolve how we use wealth. Perhaps our old framework has become outdated and no longer serves our needs individually and collectively. True wealth is built from the inside out.

Remember:

- Awareness is the key.
- Time is a factor.
- The present is perfect.
- If you do not evolve, you will become extinct - a universal truth about life. We all need to evolve; this is a new age of technology. Possibilities, collective abilities have expanded. Staying congruent means changing and evolving within our lifetimes, not between generations.
- Financial planning is a process that facilitates personal growth and evolution.
- Achieve wealth from the inside out.
- Use the energy of money intentionally to create an amazing life.
- Eliminate money problems challenges/fears/concerns for good.

Enjoy the next stage of growth - then begin by collecting the data....
The cycle begins again.

Our Wish For You

Our wish for you is that this book has awakened in you a deeper awareness of self and money. We hope you take the concepts presented in the *12 Principles for Financial Leadership* and apply them in your own lives, in your homes and in your businesses. We hope you will use your money intentionally to expand your human capital, and the human capital of every person in your family. This is the secret to sustainable wealth creation.

We wish you ultimate wealth ... we wish you the abundant joy and adventure of inspired wealth.

We endeavor to keep building and speaking on these concepts in an effort to teach financial leadership to individuals and organizations.

Please visit us at www.inspiredwealth.com where you can see what we've been up to lately. You will find a slide show about the *12 Principles for Financial*

Leadership **and get more information on what we offer groups and individuals in the way of key notes, training and coaching. We value your feedback and stories on the concepts presented in Inspired Wealth. We hope you will share your experiences with us, as they will help us continue to grow and deepen our understanding of life and money. Please email us at amiga@inpsiredwealth.com.**